THE EYE-OPENING FACTS

The Crazy and Amazing Stories Behind the World's Most Interesting Facts

Larry Baz

INTRODUCTION

Did you know that if you lift a kangaroo's tail off the ground it can't hop?

Did you know that cows have accent?

Did you know the U.S. almost went to war with Canada over a pig?

In this book, within just a few pages, you're going to learn more than you learnt from all your teachers combined.

This book is full of incredible, hilarious, and amazing things that you've never heard of before and your friends haven't either.

By showing what you'll learn in this book, you can actually wow your friends, and they'll start asking you, "Wow, really?" "Can you tell me more about that?" or even, "You are a genius, how did you know that?"

No more feeling lost for words because you've got the perfect ice breaker. This book can literally become your secret weapon in any conversation.

You can learn interesting facts about many topics, for

example:

-Countries

-Celebrities

-Movie stars

-Human body

-Science

-Economics

-Space

-Movies

-Animals

-and more, lots more.

So, let's delve into the world of the amazing and fascinating facts.

#1

The Cactus Cops Could Send You To Jail For 25 Years.

According to "The Baltimore Sun," the state of Arizona takes its cacti very seriously. A cactus has been a majestic symbol of the West for a very long time, especially one cactus in particular. The Saguaro cactus, which is tall and spiny with many arms, stands as a great symbol of the West. This is the cactus that most would visualize when they think of the good old Wild West. It's even featured on the Arizona license plates! Arizona takes the protection of this plant very seriously, which is why you could face up to 25 years in jail for cutting one down, digging it up, or harming it in any way.

The state of Arizona even has its very own plant protectors, which are also known as the cactus cops.

They are part of the Agriculture Department, and they are armed. They patrol the desert on a daily schedule protecting the Saguaro and other protected wildlife.

The Saguaro is so protected that even if it is on your own property, you need the government's permission to move it or you could face fines and jail time.

#2

There Is Honor In The War Of Soda.

When you're thirsty and looking for a cold, sugary drink, it's likely that you grab one of two highly popular drinks: Coke or Pepsi. Both of these are huge companies, and they both bring in millions of dollars each month. They are also very big competitors. You could say that these two companies are in an ongoing war with each other to see whose drink is the best. However, when it comes to war, there is such a thing as a fair and honorable opponent.

According to "The Hustle," in 2006, an employee of Coca-Cola tried to sell secrets from the company to its number one competitor, Pepsi. How did Pepsi respond to this? They told Coca-Cola that they had a leak in their company, and Coca-Cola responded by hiring an FBI agent to run an undercover operation to find the leak.

The lifeblood of Coca-Cola's success relies heavily on the amount of secrecy they have. There's a rumor that the original coke formula is kept locked away in a multi-million-dollar vault deep inside the company. Because of this extreme secrecy, only a few people were trusted with certain formulas and trade secrets.

Joya Williams was one of these people. When she

sent an email to Pepsi saying that she had a lot of classified secrets to sell to them, she thought that she was going to get away with it and live the rest of her days soaking in money. That didn't happen.

When Pepsi received the email, they forwarded it to Coca-Cola themselves, who then set up an inside investigation with an FBI agent named Gerald Reichard. Williams ended up spending eight years in jail, and Pepsi came out on top as the respectable and honorable opponent in their fierce war against Coca-Cola.

Four Have Died Searching For This Treasure.

Forrest Fenn is an eccentric man with a colorful background. He was an air force veteran when he arrived in Santa Fe, New Mexico, in the early 1970s. He became a local legend and earned himself a reputation as a treasure hunter.

He managed to gather a large collection of ancient artifacts, which he then put into an art gallery that made him $6 million annually. He appeared to have it all—the fame, the fortune, and the reputation—but then it all came crashing down when he was diagnosed with cancer.

According to "Vox," when Fenn learned that he was going to die of cancer, he put a plan in motion. He grabbed a 10-by-10-by-6-inch Romanesque chest and filled it with some of the many valuables he had accumulated over the years. He said he filled it with gold nuggets the size of chicken eggs, emeralds, pre-Columbian jewelry, diamonds, and ancient jade carvings, all of this supposedly worth $2 million. He said that he planned to drag the chest of treasure out into the Rocky Mountains and die beside it.

However, he managed to beat his cancer and left the

treasure chest to gather dust in his study.

In 2010, he decided that he wanted to leave a legacy behind for himself.

He took the treasure chest and hid it somewhere up in the Rocky Mountains and then he released a memoir called "The Thrill of the Chase," in which there is a poem explaining the location of the treasure. Four people have died searching for Forrest Fenn's treasure, and to this day, it has not been found.

Jack Daniels Died From A Broken Toe.

I bet you never thought that you could die from stubbing your toe. While it's not really possible to die of a broken toe today, it was very possible back in 1911 when Jack Daniels (the founder of the famous whiskey) died. Daniels is a very famous figure all over the world, and almost everyone has heard of or drunk his whiskey.

Even so, I bet there are very few people who know how he died.

According to "Offbeat Tennessee," Daniels arrived at his office early one morning and attempted to open his safe. Back then, safes were big, heavy, and made of iron—not something you want to kick.

Daniels did kick his safe, however, out of frustration from forgetting his combination and not being able to open it.

By kicking the safe, Daniels broke his toe. He never went to see a doctor about his broken toe and allowed it to sit and fester.

Soon, an infection developed in his broken toe, and because he left it, the infection spread to the rest of his body.

Gangrene then spread through his leg, and this resulted in it needing to be cut off to stop the infection. Daniels eventually died of blood poisoning at Lynchburg in 1911 after deeding his entire business to his nephew.

#5

One Of The Bloodiest Medieval Wars Was Fought Over A Bucket.

Throughout history, there have been many wars fought for many different reasons. Some reasons are very serious, like politics, power, economics, or just revenge. Some reasons are as simple as a difference in opinion or just not liking each other. Then there are reasons that are so stupid you wonder what was going through the minds of people at the time.

According to "The Vintage News," the "War of the Bucket" was fought between two Italian city-states, Bologna and Modena, in 1325. To fully understand why two city-states went to war over a bucket, you need to understand the history behind it. From the 12th to the 14th century, the different powers of Europe fought a series of wars, which are known as the Guelph and Ghibelline Wars. During that time, the two Italian city-states of Modena and Bologna both took opposing sides.

In 1325, a group of soldiers from Modena snuck into the city of Bologna and stole a bucket from the city's central well. It wasn't the fact that they stole the bucket that angered the people of Bologna. They were angered by the fact that their enemies were able to sneak into their city undetected and steal something. They saw it as dishonorable and demanded the return of their bucket. Modena refused to do so.

At this point, both of them should have realized that a fight over a bucket was a bit silly, but they didn't. Bologna mobilized its forces, and so did Modena. Modena was severely outnumbered during the war, and the Bolognese had the high ground. Even with these circumstances, Modena still managed to win the war and steal a second bucket from the city for good measure.

This is a funny tale, but let's not forget that 2,000 people died in this war and the Modenese soldiers destroyed most of the city of Bologna in the process. They even destroyed a sluice on the local river so that the Bolognese had no need for a bucket because they couldn't get water anymore.

#6

Stephen Hawking Threw A Party For Time Travelers.

In 2009, Stephen Hawking ran an experiment in order to prove that time travel is not possible. This experiment was highly top secret and nobody was allowed to know about it until after it was completed. This experiment took shape as a party.

According to "Mashable," Hawking threw a party for time travelers and only sent the invitations out after the party was over.

The party was equipped with balloons, champagne, food, and a smartly dressed Hawking. The event was captured and shown on the Discovery Channel. It showed Hawking all dressed up and waiting at the party for time travelers to arrive, but nobody showed up.

"I sat there for a long time, but no one came," Hawking stated to reporters at the Seattle Science Festival in 2012. He only sent out the invitations to the party after it was over. He said that this was a crucial part of the experiment.

Only a time traveler would be able to come to the party if the invitations to the party were sent out after it was over. Hawking believes that this proves that backward time travel is not possible. What if the time travelers didn't show up to the party because they're very good at keeping time travel a secret?

7

The One Place On A Cruise Ship You Don't Want To Go Is The Morgue.

People die every day, that's no secret, and there is no universal law stopping someone from dying while they are on vacation. This happens a lot more often than you think.

According to "Insider," some cruise ship workers report at least three deaths a month on cruises, and others say the number of deaths is at least three a week worldwide. The causes of death range from accidents to suicides, with the main cause being old age.

For this reason, all cruise ships are legally required to have a morgue on board and carry body bags. The morgue must be a refrigerated area kept separate from all food areas. The size of the morgue depends on the size of the ship, but the largest morgue is equipped to hold up to 10 bodies.

An ex-cruise ship employee said that if it got really bad and they didn't have enough space, they would use a walk-in freezer for the extra bodies. Let's hope that it never really gets that bad. Going on a cruise shouldn't remind you of a horror film.

#8

Birds Are The Last Surviving Dinosaurs On Earth.

Today, there are over 11,000 different species of bird, and every single one of them evolved from dinosaurs. Nearly 200 million years ago, the world was ruled by dinosaurs, both carnivores and herbivores. They were at the top of every food chain, and the birds were right there with them. This is no surprise since birds evolved from a group of meat-eating dinosaurs known as theropods. This group of dinosaurs is the same group the T-Rex belonged to; however, even back then, birds were a lot smaller than the T-Rex was.

When the end of the dinosaurs came, the conditions on the earth became very bad, and food sources grew short. Dinosaurs died out, but birds survived. Why? According to the Natural History Museum, birds had three unique advantages: their size, the type of food they ate, and the fact that they could fly.

Birds were small, even back then, and small creatures breed faster than big creatures. This meant that they could adapt to their new environment faster. The environment all over the world was changing drastically, and the birds were able to adapt to it.

Because of their small size, birds also didn't need to

eat as much as the larger dinosaurs did. This helped when food sources became scarce.

Speaking of food, birds eat a lot of it. They aren't picky with their food, and they are willing to eat anything. They will eat seeds, bugs, and even fish. Lastly, birds were some of the only dinosaurs that could fly. Flying is faster and uses less energy than walking or running.

This means that when disaster struck, the birds were able to fly away and find a safe place and food more easily than the other dinosaurs.

These three reasons are why birds are the only surviving dinosaurs today. Maybe we should all learn to fly, just in case.

#9

A Bullet Cured Mental Illness.

A man, who is identified only as George, tried to commit suicide when he was only 19 years old. He was unhappy with his life because of his mental illnesses. George had OCD (obsessive compulsive disorder), and he had an extreme dislike of germs.

According to "The New York Times," George washed his hands more than a hundred times a day and took showers frequently. This uncontrollable behavior caused George to quit his job and drop out of school.

The doctor who was treating George, Dr. Solyom, had treated George for years before he attempted to kill himself. Dr. Solyom said that George once told his mother that his life was wretched and he wished he was dead. To this, his mother replied, "So look, George, if your life is so wretched, just go and shoot yourself."

That is what George did. He went down to the basement, put a .22 caliber gun inside his mouth, and shot himself.

The bullet didn't kill George. It lodged itself in the left frontal lobe of his brain where the mental illness that was ruining his life was located. After the operation that removed the bullet from his brain, George was transferred to another hospital. It didn't take them long to realize that his usually obsessive compulsive behavior was gone. George didn't have the need to wash his hands or shower at all.

The bullet had destroyed the part of the brain causing his mental illness without damaging any other part of his brain. George went back to school and got a brand-new job. His life is far better today than it was when he had his illness.

#10
A Hot Magnet Is No Longer A Good Magnet.

Magnets are very useful objects because of their ability to create a constant magnetic field, and they are used in many things from phones to cars. However, a magnet isn't completely strong and unchangeable as its magnetic field can be affected by something as simple as a change in temperature. If you ask "Apex Magnets," they'll tell you that they've done many experiments with magnets. These experiments prove that a magnet will lose the strength of its magnetism if it is exposed to extreme heat.

A magnet is made up of atoms, as most things are. In a normal environment with normal temperatures, the atoms of a magnet align perfectly, which creates a field of magnetism. When a magnet is heated up, the particles in the magnet are forced to move around really fast. This confuses the atoms and causes them to no longer be aligned, which, in turn, affects the strength of the magnetic field. You can imagine that the opposite would happen if you put a magnet in a freezer. If you want a super magnet, I would suggest giving that a try.

#11
Female Cats Are Right-Handed.

As humans, we are identified as being either left-handed or right-handed. This means that we prefer using a specific hand for things like writing, throwing, and catching. According to new research and "Science Alert," it's not just humans that do this.

Just like you would prefer to use your right hand to write with, a female cat would prefer to use her right paw to reach for food or walk down steps. A male cat prefers to use his left paw to do the same. With humans, a preference in handedness isn't specific to gender, but with cats, this doesn't seem to be the case. Which paw they prefer to use seems to be completely gender-specific. Most female cats prefer their right paw, and most male cats prefer their left paw. Something like this has never been witnessed in the animal kingdom before.

#12

A Bolt Of Lightning Is Hotter Than The Surface Of The Sun.

According to "Seeker," a bolt of lightning is actually a lot hotter than the surface of the Sun. In fact, it is more than three times hotter. The surface of the Sun is as hot as 10,340 degrees Fahrenheit.

A single bolt of lightning can be as hot as 53,540 degrees Fahrenheit.

However, it's important to note that the surface of the Sun is the coldest part of the Sun.

The Sun's core is as hot as 27 million degrees Fahrenheit, and the atmosphere above the surface of the Sun can exceed 900,000 degrees Fahrenheit.

A physics professor at the University of Washington, Robert H. Holzworth, said that power is the rate at which energy is used. Power is energy per second.

The energy per second in lightning is far higher than the energy per second on the surface of the Sun.

Therefore, a bolt of lightning has more power than the surface of the Sun, but that energy only lasts for a few seconds, whereas the energy from the surface of the Sun lasts for longer.

The overall energy of the Sun is far higher than the overall energy of a lightning bolt, but the lightning bolt is able to dissipate that energy a lot faster than the Sun is.

#13

The 25 Year Search For The Loch Ness Monster.

Steve Feltham gave up his home and his job in Dorset to move to a place named Dores, which is near Inverness. He did all this because of his passion to find or at least spot the Loch Ness monster. He began searching in 1991, but he says that he has been fascinated by the mystery of the monster since he was a child.

According to "BBC News," his search for the Loch Ness monster is recognized by the *Guinness Book of World Records* as the longest, most continuous monster-hunting vigil of Loch Ness. He spent 25 years of his life staying in one spot, hoping to catch a glimpse of the famous monster of the loch.

Feltham admitted that he had hoped to finish his search in the first three years of leaving his home and his job. However, now after spending 25 years searching for the Loch Ness monster, he says that he is willing to dedicate another 25 years of his life to this search.

In his time searching, Feltham said that he had one sighting of something that he could not explain, but even he couldn't say what it was.

#14
The Only Town In The U.S. With A Population Of 1.

In Nebraska, there is a small town five miles from the South Dakota border. It is in a remote part of the state, and it is called Monowi. You can see the entirety of the town just by climbing on top of a rock and having a look around.

There are abandoned buildings, things falling apart, and overgrown grass and weeds that are a sign that nature is taking this place back for itself.

From the outside, this place would look like a ghost town. However, this ghost town has a mayor, a bartender, a librarian, and a clerk, and she is the only soul living there.

Elsie Eiler wasn't always the only occupant of the town. Her husband, Rudy, passed away in 2004, which officially made her the only resident of the smallest town in the United States.

According to "BBC News," this town of Monowi is the only place in the United States with a population of 1.

This place didn't always use to be this way. In the 1930s, it was a bustling town that all kinds of tourists stopped at. Eiler grew up there, and she says that there is no way that she is leaving.

If you go to visit the town, be sure to look out for the sign that reads: "Welcome to The World Famous Monowi Tavern. Coldest Beers in Town!"

#15
The Reason Teachers Don't Want You Chewing Gum In Class.

New research has shown that chewing gum just before taking a test can improve your test scores. This may explain why teachers always tell you to spit out your gum while in class. They know somehow! In all seriousness, this research is fairly new, but it has shown quite a lot of evidence that a person's brainpower is increased directly after chewing a piece of gum. According to "Live Science," researchers believe that the improvement in brain function is because the action of chewing gum actually warms up the brain.

It also increases heart rate and blood pressure, which, in turn, increases the flow of blood to the brain. This directly affects your brainpower. However, most of the tests show that chewing gum only increases brain power for 15 to 20 minutes total; after that, brain functions start dropping back down to normal.

Research also shows that it is better to chew gum right before taking a test and not during or even a few minutes before a test. I don't know if the flavor of the gum matters, but it would be interesting if it did.

#16
Would You Like A Toe In Your Drink?

The Sourtoe Cocktail has become a famous tradition in the city of Dawson. This cocktail was first established in 1973, and it consists of a human toe that has been amputated, dehydrated, and preserved in salt and used to garnish any drink of your choosing. It sounds disgusting, but the drink has already been tried by over 60,000 people.

According to "Atlas Obscura," the drink was created in 1973 by a Yukon local named Captain Dick Stevenson. The first toe used in the creation of this drink belonged to a miner and rum runner by the name of Louie Liken.

He lost his toe due to frostbite in the 1920s but kept it preserved in a jar of alcohol for the memories. Captain Stevenson found the toe almost 50 years later still preserved in the jar.

He took the toe down to the Sourdough Saloon and started putting it into people's drinks and daring anyone who was brave enough to drink it. That was the creation of the Sourtoe Cocktail.

The original toe was used in the drink for a further seven years. Unfortunately, in 1980, Garry Younger, a miner, was drinking his 13th glass of Sourtoe champagne when his chair tipped backward. Garry fell over and accidentally swallowed the original toe, and it was never recovered. However, since then, seven more toes have been donated to the bar, and the tradition continues.

According to the locals, if you go into this bar, there is only one rule: "You can drink it fast, you can drink it slow, but the lips have to touch the toe."

#17
The Slowest News Day In History.

There are so many different ways for us to keep in contact with the world these days. There's always some kind of news to hear from some part of the world.

We can always rely on our phones, laptops, computers, and car radios to keep us informed.

However, in 1930, the only way you would be able to hear the news was if you had an old-fashioned radio on the counter in your kitchen or living room.

April 18, 1930, was the slowest news day in history for one reason. When everyone in the U.K. turned on their radios and sat down to listen to the daily news report, they heard something that we would never hear today.

According to "BBC News," a news announcer got on the radio, as he was supposed to do every day, and simply said: "There is no news."

After that, the rest of what was supposed to be a 15-minute news segment was filled with 15 minutes of piano music. We will never forget the slowest news day in history since there will probably never be another one like it in this day and age.

An Accidental Evacuation Leads To Little Response.

We all make mistakes sometimes. It's a normal part of human life after all. However, there are some mistakes that are so big that you have to wonder if they can even be classified as a mistake any more.

One such incident happened in 2005 in Connecticut. According to "Insider," there was supposed to be a test of the Emergency Alert System on that day, but someone must have pressed the wrong button.

Before anyone knew what was happening, television and radio signals were hijacked by an emergency broadcast. The broadcast said that all of the residents needed to evacuate, but it didn't give any reason as to why they needed to evacuate.

Not long after the emergency alert was issued, it was recalled and deemed a false alarm.

Kerry Flaherty, from the Office of Emergency Management, told "NBC News" that there was no need for an evacuation and there was no state emergency. She said, "It was an erroneous message."

Although the emergency alert to evacuate was false,

only one percent of the population actually prepared to evacuate. If it was a real emergency, only that one percent would have survived. They're the smart ones, if you ask me.

#19
When We're Born, We're Only Afraid Of Two Things.

Fear is adaptive. We aren't born scared of all the things we are scared of now. Fear is something we learn. It's how humans have survived for so long. We learn to be afraid of things, and that fear helps us survive against predators and other things that could harm us.

When we are born, we only have two innate fears. We are born with these two fears because they are necessary for our survival as a species.

According to "CNN Health," these two fears are fear of falling and fear of loud sounds.

There have been many studies done on infants, both human and animal, to determine these fears from a young age.

The fear of falling and the fear of loud sounds are necessary for any species' survival. When placed on a high surface that was half solid and half plexiglass, most of the infants stayed clear of the plexiglass as they saw it as the edge of a cliff.

They thought that they would fall off if they went toward the glass, so they stayed away from it.

Loud sounds are usually an indication that there is danger nearby. When most people hear a loud sound, they experience a fight or flight response. This is why we are prone to ducking for cover or jumping up when there is a loud sound. We are either preparing to fight or getting ready to run.

The First *Harry Potter* Book Was Rejected 12 Times.

If you ever thought that being an author was easy, think again. Some of the most famous books published today were never thought to be good back when they were first written. There are many examples of this happening, but we only have to look at one. J.K. Rowling's original synopsis of her book *Harry Potter and the Sorcerer's Stone* is just the first book in a long series of books that are loved worldwide. However, getting her book accepted by a publishing agency was not an easy task.

According to "Insider," J.K. Rowling typed out a one-page synopsis in 1995 to accompany the opening chapters of her book. She then presented it to several publishing agencies, all of which rejected her. All of them were too scared to take a chance on an unknown female author, no matter how good the actual content of the book was. She was rejected by a total of 12 publishing houses before her book was finally accepted by Bloomsbury. I bet those 12 publishing houses are kicking themselves for letting a diamond in the rough like *Harry Potter* slip through their fingers.

#21
Can You Imagine Only Having One Toe?

Every species is born with the things it needs to help it survive in this world. Humans are born with toes on our feet to help us balance and grip the floor while we walk or run. If we didn't have five toes on each foot, we would have trouble balancing, walking, and running.

Zebras are close relatives to horses, and just like horses, they are born to run. According to *The Wild World of Zoo Books*, even a zebra who is only an hour old can run as fast as it needs to in order to keep up with its herd. A zebra can run up to 35 miles an hour, and it's all thanks to the way it was born: Its long, strong legs, and its one toe. Yes, zebras only have one toe on each foot. The toe is surrounded by a hard hoof. The fact that they have one toe, narrow feet, and hard hooves is why the zebras cannot only run really fast but can also run on hard surfaces that would hurt other animals' feet.

Zebras need to be able to outrun predators like lions, so it's important that they are able to run fast and across surfaces that other animals can't run on. Zebras also stand out in the field and graze all day, so the strength of their legs and feet is also important for that. It might sound weird, but having only one toe is a biological advantage for them.

#22
Sea Otters Hold Hands So They Don't Float Away.

This might just be the cutest sight you will ever see. According to "Mother Nature Network," sea otters like to hold hands while they are sleeping.

You've probably seen a picture of otters holding hands while floating in the water as there are several of them circling the internet. You might have thought it was a lucky photo and that something like this probably doesn't happen very often, but it actually does.

Otters do like to hold each other's hands but usually only while they are sleeping.

When otters sleep, they float on their backs on the surface of the water. Otters will hold each other's hands so that they don't float away from each other while they are asleep. I know what you're thinking: "That is so cute!" It's mostly a mother otter and her pup that will hold hands to keep from floating away from each other. Otters are also known to use sea kelp to keep from floating away. The kelp is attached to the seafloor and then wrapped around the otter. It acts as an anchor while they are sleeping, but it's a lot cuter when they're holding hands.

#23

Be Nice To Bees, They Can Recognize Your Face.

According to "Science Daily," a student from Monash University named Adrian Dyer has trained a bee to recognize and distinguish between human faces. There is no biological need for a bee to be able to do this. They can go about their day-to-day tasks without ever needing to recognize one human face from another. Yet, in 2005, Dyer taught a bee to do just that by associating pictures of human faces with sugary snacks. However, Martin Giurfa, a student from the Université de Toulouse in France, thought that the bees didn't recognize the human faces but rather lines and patterns of those faces.

Of course, Adrian was right, and further studies proved that the bees were able to distinguish one human face from another. However, they used the patterns, lines, and dots of each face in order to tell each one apart from another. They were able to see that one face had a unique pattern. It was as if the bees were seeing each human face as a unique flower. They are able to see the position of the features on our face (i.e. eyes, cheeks, lips, nose, etc.) and use those features to distinguish one face from another. This is probably the same strategy they use to identify and recognize different objects in their environment. It's also good to keep in mind that most of these studies were done on honeybees.

The moral of the story is that you should be nice to a bee because the next time one sees you, it might be able to recognize you. You don't want a bee to sting you out of revenge, do you?

#24

Get Out Your Torches For Snowman Burning Day.

Snowman Burning Day takes place on March 20 each year at Lake Superior. According to "The Fact Site," Lake Superior is thought to be one of the coldest places in the country, which is why Snowman Burning Day is so important to the people in the area. It's a day they use to celebrate the end of winter and the start of spring. They burn snowmen to celebrate the end of the cold.

In reality, they aren't burning actual snowmen. Their snowmen are made of wood, straw, paper, and wire and decorated to resemble a snowman, and they are about 3 meters tall.

Sometimes, the snowmen are made to look like people.

It all started in 1971 on March 20 at Lake Superior State University. A former campus club, known as the Unicorn Hunters, came up with the idea of Snowman Burning Day. They were inspired by the "Rose Sunday Festival" that is celebrated in Germany.

During this festival, the mayor would walk through the town with a straw snowman.

If the children of the town had been good, he would burn the snowman for them.

Snowman Burning Day is a huge celebration. It has turned into a huge festival with good food, poetry, and one of the biggest fires of any celebration year-round.

#25

Did You Know That Santa Claus Has A Pilot's License?

In 1927, Santa Claus received his pilot's license from the U.S. government at the Commerce Department in Washington. A photo was taken of it being handed to him by the Assistant Secretary of Commerce at the time. According to "Did You Know Stuff," along with his pilot's license, Santa also received some airway maps and a promise that the runway lights would be kept on all night long on Christmas Eve so that Santa would never have a problem delivering all his presents.

Santa Claus also went back to renew his license and passed an eye examination and health check not too long ago. He was cleared to fly, despite the fact that his blood sugar levels were too high from all the milk and cookies he eats. He was given a new license by Marc Garneau, a former astronaut. You can rest easy knowing that Santa will always be able to deliver those presents just in time for Christmas.

#26
In Russia, Eating Ice Cream Can Keep You Warm.

Russian folklore will have you believe that because it's usually so cold in Russia, eating ice cream can actually warm you up.

According to "The Edmonton Journal," the normal air temperature in Russia is so low that eating ice cream does actually raise your body temperature.

If it's -40 degrees outside and your ice cream is only -5 degrees, then you can see how eating some ice cream would be able to keep you warm.

Russians have plenty of other beliefs about the cold. One belief is that if you complain about the winter, you are being unpatriotic. The extremely cold winters in Russia are the reason they were able to defend against two major invasions during World War II.

They were used to the cold, but their enemies weren't. Therefore, to complain about the cold is to be unpatriotic. Another belief is that it's unmanly to put down the earflaps of the big fur hats many Russian men wear to keep warm.

#27
Ronald MacDonald Robbed Wendy's!

No, not the Ronald McDonald clown we all know and love from McDonald's. A man named Ronald MacDonald, who was 22 years old, had been working at a Wendy's in Manchester, England, for quite some time. You would think a man with that name working at Wendy's was bad enough, but what's even worse is that he tried to steal money from them.

According to "Foster," early on a Monday morning, the manager of Wendy's called the police and reported the robbery. MacDonald and his accomplice, Steve Lemay, were taking money out of the Wendy's safe at 1:30 a.m.

They were both detained at the store and then arrested when the police arrived. I guess Ronald might have been better off working as a clown.

Free Rubber Duckies For Everybody!

According to "Mother Nature Network," in 1992, a shipping crate that contained a total of 28,000 rubber ducks fell overboard and was lost at sea. The ship they were on had just left Hong Kong and was on its way to the United States at the time. When this happened, it was ignored as an unfortunate accident. However, over 20 years later, these plastic bath toys are still circulating the ocean's currents and popping up on beaches all over the world.

Since they started their journey in 1992, the ducks have shown up on beaches in South America, Alaska, Australia, and even Hawaii. Some of the ducks have even been found in the Arctic ice, frozen. A few of the ducks have made it as far as the Atlantic

Ocean and Scotland.

These rubber ducks have become so popular that they've gathered a massive following of fans. Each one of the fans is eager to take and share photos of the ducks and track their progress across the ocean. They're so cute, I want to take one home with me.

#29
Cold Can Make You Lose Weight.

It sounds hard to believe, but it's true. According to "MSN Lifestyle," having a cold shower not only promotes weight loss but comes with several other benefits as well. Cold showers can also lower stress levels, improve sleep quality, create better blood circulation, increase testosterone levels, and improve fertility. Having a cold shower, either in the morning or in the evening, can be difficult to do as most people prefer the relaxing feeling of hot, steamy water. However, if you're willing to grin and bear it, you'll receive so many more benefits from having a quick cold shower.

Cold showers can boost your metabolism, increase your blood flow, and increase the activity of your brown fat, which helps your body burn calories in order to keep your body warm. Overall, next time you hop into the shower, it's better to turn the water to cold.

#30

The Length Of Your Yawn Equals The Size Of Your Brain.

Scientists have noticed that larger animals, such as hippos, gorillas, and elephants, who have larger bodies than humans but proportionately smaller brains, yawn for a shorter time than humans. It used to be believed that the larger the body, the longer the yawn. However, this new observation changes that thinking.

Scientists are now suggesting that the size of your brain and the number of active neurons firing in your brain is directly linked to the length of your yawn.

According to "Science Alert," some researchers from State University of New York were scanning YouTube for videos of animals yawning. In the end, they studied over 205 yawns. They were able to determine that humans had the longest yawn, which lasts up to 6.5 seconds. They also realized that the size and shape of an animal's body or jaw did not directly affect the length or strength of their yawns.

The only possible factor was the size of their brains, which makes sense because it's thought that our brains are what make us yawn.

#31
Pinocchio Has A Paradox.

We all know about the famous tale of the puppet Pinocchio. He melted everyone's heart with his perilous journey that turned him into a real boy. We also know about his unfortunate dilemma: He can't lie without his nose growing twice its size. I bet not everyone knows about a small, but funny fact involving Pinocchio's nose.

If Pinocchio said, "My nose will grow now," then he would be creating a paradox. A paradox is kind of like a hiccup in time. You see, Pinocchio's nose grows whenever he is lying. If he says that his nose is going to grow, then he is both lying and not lying, so then his nose will both grow and not grow. That is a paradox. By saying that his nose will grow, he is lying, so then his nose must grow, but if his nose grows, then he is no longer lying, so then it can't grow. I don't know about you, but I would have liked to see this mentioned in the movie.

#32

Forgetful Squirrels Are Helping Build Forests.

According to "Science NetLinks," squirrels are forgetting where they bury their nuts, and it's actually helping build up our forests. To be more specific, grey squirrels are the forgetful ones.

You've probably seen them around the neighborhood park or in your backyard. They are actually forest-dwelling animals, and up until recently, they were helping to grow the forests.

Wildlife ecologist Rob Swihart from Purdue University said that squirrels are the most important species when it comes to the spread of acorns.

He said that acorns rely on either gravity or squirrels to spread to new areas and grow into trees. The grey squirrel, in particular, is heavily responsible for this.

Grey squirrels bury their nuts in the ground in multiple areas, and they end up forgetting where they've buried them.

A grey squirrel will forget where it's buried about 50 percent of its nuts. These nuts eventually take root and grow into new trees.

This forgetful practice is opposed to the red squirrels that store their nuts in a pile above ground. Those nuts dry out and never take root, so they can never grow into new trees.

Thumbs-up to grey squirrels for helping the environment!

#33

Hawaiians Didn't Invent The Hawaiian Pizza.

Hawaiian pizza is one of the most debated things on the internet today. There are numerous haters of the pizza topping, as well as plenty of pineapple lovers to back the topping.

However, how many people know that their beloved or hated Hawaiian pizza is not actually Hawaiian?

This pizza topping that has put a wedge between pizza lovers for years was invented in 1962. A Greek man named Sam Panopoulos moved to Canada and opened up a restaurant.

This was around the same time that the pizza craze was only just spreading through America, and the young Greek-Canadian restaurant owner knew it would spread to Canada soon.

According to "The Vintage News," Sam first decided to put canned pineapple on pizza as a "fun experiment." Nobody actually liked the pizza at first, but it quickly caught on and became one of the biggest topics of debate today.

Sam named the pizza Hawaiian Pizza, not because it is Hawaiian, but because that was the name of the canned pineapples that he used.

Sam died on June 8, 2017, but he left a mark on this world and opened us all up to new and exciting flavors.

#34
Kids Ask A Lot Of Questions.

You know what they say: Curiosity killed the cat. Well, children don't know this saying, nor do they live by it. Children are extremely curious.

According to the "Hindustan Times," children ask an average of 300 questions a day. That's a lot of information to get at once, assuming that all of those questions were answered. A few studies were done and the results showed that young children ask between 288 and 300 questions a day.

These results were dependent on their age and gender. Girls who are 4 years old ask the most questions, up to 390 a day! Also, 24 percent of the children were more likely to go to their mothers to ask a question rather than their fathers.

Some would think that children ask so many questions because of a survival instinct that has helped ensure the future of the human race. This isn't entirely true. Children ask questions because they are simply curious and they don't yet know how most of the world works.

#35

It's Raining Fish! No, It's Just A Tornado.

It may sound strange, and it is, but it does actually rain fish. This is a very rare occurrence, but if the circumstances are right, then it does happen. The main culprit for the phenomenon is tornadoes.

It doesn't actually rain fish the same way as it rains water. The fish are just taken from the sea, or sometimes a lake, and repositioned in the air.

According to "Science Questions with Surprising Answers," it happens when a tornado moves over a body of water and becomes what is known as a waterspout.

A waterspout sucks up the water and anything in the water, including the fish or other creatures that could be swimming around.

What the waterspout sucks up then travels up the tornado's vortex and blows around in the clouds for a while.

When the tornado loses its energy and starts to dissipate, the air that is keeping the fish in the clouds disappears. When that happens, the fish start to rain down. Sometimes, the fish rain down miles away from where they were picked up.

This doesn't just happen with fish; snakes, frogs, worms, and even squid and alligators have been known to rain from the sky before.

#36

The Eiffel Tower Is Taller In The Summer Than In The Winter.

I bet you didn't know that the Eiffel Tower grows in the summer and shrinks in the winter. Well, it does. If you're planning on going to Paris, you should go in the summertime, that way when you go to the top of the Eiffel Tower, it will be taller and you can see more.

To go into specifics, the Eiffel Tower can actually grow up to six inches in the summer and shrink back down during the winter.

You may be asking why it would do this. The answer is pretty simple if you remember the fact that the Eiffel Tower is made of steel.

According to "IP Factly," steel, like most metals, has the ability to expand and contract depending on temperature changes.

When certain metals get hot, they tend to expand, and when they get cold, they contract.

This is what is happening with the Eiffel Tower. In the summer, the temperatures get so hot that the steel of the Eiffel Tower is forced to expand. In the winter, the temperatures drop back down, and the steel contracts again.

The Eiffel Tower might be able to grow taller in hotter temperatures, but it's unable to grow any more than six inches, and it can't shrink lower than its normal size when it's cold.

#37

You Should Always Wash Your Food, Just Like Boars Do.

Pigs are usually made out to be dirty and disgusting creatures. A widely known insult, "eating like a pig," is meant to disgrace someone and let them know that they are a slob and they're eating like one.

However, what if not all pigs acted the way we think pigs act?

According to "National Geographic," researchers have seen several wild boars in different instances taking their dirty food down to the water and cleaning it.

It all started when a zoo employee at the Basel Zoo in Switzerland witnessed the zoo's wild boars taking dirty apple chunks down to the water and cleaning them before chowing down. This revelation was followed up by several experiments.

Researchers from the University College London joined the Basel Zoo to do these experiments. They were able to determine that pigs could tell when their food was dirty.

Instead of eating straight away, the pigs would drag their food to a water source, slosh it around a bit to make sure it was clean, and then eat it. Pigs are known to be extremely intelligent creatures with an ability to quickly adapt to their environment.

Therefore, this kind of behavior should be expected from such an intelligent creature, but this was the first actual sighting of them washing their food before eating it.

#38

Hippopotomonstrosesquippedalioph obia

That is a very long and complicated word. According to "Fear Of," this is the scientific name given to the fear or phobia of long words. Yes, you read that right. This very long and hard-to-pronounce word is used to describe people who have a fear of long words.

There are a lot of phobias and fears around today. You might think some of them are joke-worthy and ridiculous, but make no mistake, these are real fears.

Today, people have managed to create a fear or phobia of almost anything, including long words. People who are suffering from this phobia aren't scared of long words in the way you might think.

They won't let out a bloodcurdling scream and run for the hills if they see a long word. Instead, when they are faced with a long word, they experience a great deal of anxiety. It's extremely ironic and kind of funny that the word used to describe people with this fear is such a long one.

This phobia is a weird one, but it can be explained. Usually, someone with a fear of long words is afraid because of an event that was possibly traumatizing to them.

Certain parts of the brain associated long words with the event and blamed those words.

This causes the person to see long words as dangerous or deadly to them. No one is born this way, and most don't even remember how their fear of long words even started.

#39
Tears Are A Really Big Turnoff.

Female tears, in particular, are a really big turnoff for men. According to "Nature," the tears that women shed contain chemicals in them. These chemicals act as signals to men, and they decrease the testosterone levels and their sexual arousal. These chemicals are called pheromones. The existence of pheromones in humans has been a highly debated subject for a while now.

Some research has shown that human sweat, which also fits into the category of pheromones, does communicate information to others through the chemicals that are released into the air. This includes information about emotional states. It is believed that human tears do the same thing.

If women's tears can lower the testosterone levels in men, then this can be seen as a survival technique. Testosterone is directly linked to aggression levels. If women's tears can lower a man's testosterone levels, then it's safe to believe that they can lower their aggression levels as well. This could be a piece in the evolutionary puzzle.

#40
The Tree Of Death Actually Exists.

The tree known as "The Tree of Death" is exactly what it sounds like. Its actual name is the Manchineel tree, and you can find it in a lot of places.

The Caribbean, South America, the Gulf of Mexico, Florida, the Bahamas, and the Galapagos Islands are all home to the Manchineel tree. Why is it known as "The Tree of Death"? The answer to that is simple: Every part of this tree is very deadly to humans. The leaves, the bark, the sap, and the fruit of this tree contain a lot of toxins, mainly the organic compound known as phorbol. This compound can be found in every single part of the tree.

Just touching the bark of the tree can leave severe chemical burns on your skin. The most dangerous part of the tree is the apple-like fruit that grows on it.

According to "IFL Science," eating the fruit can cause seizures, severe vomiting, diarrhea, and, in some cases, death. If you try to burn this tree, the smoke it releases into the air will cause severe irritation in your eyes and, in some cases, temporary blindness. All in all, this is a tree from hell, despite the fact that it can be mostly found on tourist-friendly beaches and iguanas seem to like them.

#41

Making Your Baby Cry Is Good Luck In Japan.

Specifically, if a Sumo wrestler makes your baby cry, it is considered a sign of good luck and good health in Japan. According to "Insider," this is part of a 400-year-old tradition that takes place in a ceremony. This ceremony is performed at various shrines all over the nation, and it's a pretty big thing.

During the ceremony, mothers watch gleefully as Sumo wrestlers try their hardest to make the baby cry. Some wrestlers will even roar in the baby's face in order to produce some tears. When the baby cries, the sound is supposed to reach God, and then the parents hope that God will give their baby good health and good luck in its life.

Therefore, it's extremely important that those Sumo wrestlers make those babies cry out as loud as they can. In general, this isn't a competition with winners or losers, although that sometimes depends on where you go. In some places, the last baby to cry is seen as the loser, while in other places, the first baby to cry is considered the loser. It's kind of strange, but if it gives the babies good luck, then why not?

#42

Tin Cans Were Invented 48 Years Before Can Openers Were.

In 1810, a man from England named Peter Durand filed the first patent for the cans used to store food in. The can was made of thick wrought iron, about 3/16 of an inch thick, with tin lining. Interestingly, the first device made specifically for opening these cans was designed and created almost 50 years later.

According to "Connecticut History," the first can opener was invented on January 5, 1858, by Ezra J. Warner, from Waterbury, U.S. It was a pointed blade that could pierce into the middle of the top of the can with a guard that stopped it from piercing too deep. Then the guard was removed and a second blade swung down. The second blade could then carve through the edges of the can in a saw-like action.

At this point, the thick wrought-iron cans were being replaced by thinner steel cans. However, until the creation of the can opener, people were told to use a hammer and chisel to cut open the top of the can. You can imagine it was probably a really long time before anyone got to eat their baked beans.

In Canada, It's Illegal To Use An Apology As An Admission Of Guilt.

We all know that Canadians love to say "sorry." They say it a lot without actually needing to. Sometimes, they just say it because they want to. Did you know that because Canadians say sorry so often, a law had to be passed called the "Apology Act"? According to "The Loop" in the province of Ontario, the "Apology Act" was passed in 2009 because of the overuse of the word "sorry" in Canada.

In some cases, an apology can be an admission of guilt. If you didn't do anything wrong but for some reason, you apologized for the incident, as a Canadian would do, then you could be legally admitting your guilt to the incident. You can see how this would cause major problems in Canada where the word "sorry" is used so freely. That's why the "Apology Act" was passed.

With this act, in Ontario, apologizing can no longer be used as an admission of guilt. Now Canadians can apologize to their heart's content without worrying about admitting to guilt.

#44
Volcanoes On The Moon!

You would think that after all of this time, we would know everything there is to know about the Moon. We've sent so many satellites and probes to the Moon, not to mention we've had humans themselves walking on the surface of the Moon.

Yet, we've just learned something new that could make geologists re-write all of the books that were written about the Moon.

According to "Space.com," there may have been active, erupting volcanoes on the Moon around the same time as there were dinosaurs on Earth. Up until now, it was thought that the volcanoes on the Moon became inactive over a billion years ago. This new evidence shows that the volcanoes were probably active as recently as 50 million years ago.

Some photos taken by the LRO spacecraft show several distinctive rock deposits that suggest volcanic activity that was very widespread. Three of the rock deposits are thought to be no older than 100 million years.

One deposit, called Ina, might only be 50 million years old. The timelines of these rock deposits prove that while dinosaurs were still on Earth, volcanoes were erupting on the Moon!

#45

There's A Name For The Offspring Of A Polar Bear And A Grizzly Bear.

Prizzly bear is the name given to the hybrid offspring of a polar bear and a grizzly bear, although they also go by the name grolar bear or nanulak. Grizzly bears and polar bears are very different creatures; from their habits to the environments they occupy, they are almost opposites. Despite the differences in the way they live, polar bears and grizzly bears are actually similar genetically. However, they tend to avoid each other out in the wild for multiple reasons, but global warming and the melting of the ice caps might be forcing these two creatures closer together.

According to "The Sun," prizzly bears have been showing up out of nowhere. One such sighting was in 2006 by hunter Jim Martell. He shot the bear, suspecting it to be a polar bear, but some officials believed it showed some grizzly bear traits. Further DNA testing confirmed the bear to be a hybrid from a polar bear mother and a grizzly bear father.

#46

Two Ais Were Shut Down After They Created Their Own Language.

Facebook created two artificial intelligence chatbots in an attempt to launch an experiment. However, the experiment was shut down after the chatbots developed a language of their own that only they could understand.

According to the "Independent," this all started when Facebook challenged these chatbots to try and negotiate a trade with each other. The AI chatbots were asked to swap things such as balls, books, and hats that were all given a certain value. Facebook wanted to see if the chatbots could recognize what value an object had and properly negotiate with one another in order to trade items.

Facebook hoped that the chatbots would be able to negotiate among themselves and that eventually, their bartering skills would improve.

However, that was not what they got. Shortly after the start of the experiment, the AI chatbots developed their own kind of language that was based on shorthand English. The words they were using were English, but they were arranged in a way that made no sense to anyone else but the chatbots. The chatbots still managed to settle negotiations and successfully trade with each other in this strange language that no one could understand.

Facebook insists that they shut down the experiment not because they were afraid of the chatbots but because they wanted a chatbot that could communicate with humans and these ones couldn't.

#47

Leonardo DiCaprio's Famous Line in *Titanic* Was Improvised.

The movie *Titanic* is a classic that we have all probably watched more times than we care to mention. On the surface, it's a three-hour film about a sinking ship.

For those that have looked deeper, it is a work of art and worthy of the real-life tale behind it.

Today, it is famous for its feelings of nostalgia and its many memorable quotes. According to "Teen Vogue," one of the most famous and memorable lines in the film almost didn't make it into the final cut.

One of Leonardo DiCaprio's most famous lines takes place while standing on the bow of the ship when he throws out his arms and shouts, "I'm the king of the world!"

That line wasn't even in the script! James Cameron, the director of the film, made it up on the spot. He said that they were trying several lines between the two characters in the scene, and it just wasn't working.

Eventually, the talented director told Leo to throw his arms out and shout "I'm the king of the world" while just loving the moment.

At first, Leo himself wasn't sure about the line, but he managed to pull it off, and thank goodness that he did. The movie just wouldn't be the same without that one line.

#48

Fukushima Has Bought 10,000 Packets Of Sunflower Seeds.

There have been some horrible nuclear disasters in certain parts of the world, from the horror that happened in Chernobyl to the disaster in Fukushima.

Both disasters left those areas uninhabitable and kept many people busy for years cleaning up what remained of the nuclear contamination. Thankfully, scientists have discovered some things that can help with this cleanup, including sunflowers.

According to "Japan Today," the idea was first tested in the mid-1990s in Chernobyl. Michael Blaylcok, a soil scientist who worked on the sunflower project in Chernobyl, explained the science behind it. He said that sunflowers are really good at taking up the radioactive isotopes.

The plant takes in the radiation in the ground and uses it to grow, and as it grows, it sucks up more and more isotopes. The sunflower can't tell the difference between the nutrients it needs to grow and the radioactive isotopes, which is very helpful when it comes to cleaning the radioactive isotopes out of the water and soil in places like Fukushima.

#49
In The Future, African Elephants Might Not Have Tusks.

From 1977 to 1992, the country of Mozambique was in the clutches of a civil war. This war was against poachers after African elephants, and it lasted for 15 years and killed nearly 90 percent of the species, all of them slaughtered for their ivory tusks and meat. Some of the oldest elephants that live in Mozambique's Gorongosa National Park still bear unmistakable scars from this civil war—that is, many of them have no tusks.

According to "National Geographic," about a third of the female elephant generation born after the war did not develop tusks. Up until the civil war, only 2 to 4 percent of female elephants were born without tusks. During the war, the few elephants who were tuskless had a biological advantage over those who had tusks.

The hunters had no need to go for the elephants without tusks, so they were left unharmed. Since then, 51 percent of the elephants that survived the war are tuskless and 32 percent of the female elephants born are also tuskless. Elephants are evolving to be tuskless in order to combat the poaching themselves.

An Italian Banker Became A Modern-Day Robin Hood.

In 2009, the world was caught in the middle of a financial crisis. Small towns like Forni di Sopra, an Italian town with a population of 1,100 people, were struggling more than others.

This small town, in particular, was on the edge of bankruptcy. The bank manager in this small town, Gilberto Baschiera, could not let himself stand by and watch as some people suffered more than others.

According to "The Washington Post," the bank manager could no longer justify rejecting requests for loans from the residents of his town who were far too poor to qualify. He decided to take matters into his own hands.

Gilberto set up a system where he would take money from the accounts of the wealthier clients and divert the money into the accounts of their poor clients. This was so they could qualify for the loans that they needed. Over the course of seven years, he managed to divert 1 million euros, or $1.15 million.

In 2016, his scheme broke down as the people who he gave the loans to were unable to pay the bank back. Gilberto was deemed a hero and called a "modern Robin Hood" by some, but this was not how the authorities saw it.

Gilberto was sentenced to two years in prison because it was determined that he didn't directly benefit from the scheme.

However, this modern-day Robin Hood won't be spending any time in jail due to the Italian law allowing courts to show leniency to someone who is a first-time offender and is given a very light sentence.

#51

The Longest War In History Lasted Over 600 Years.

Thousands of years ago, the ancient Romans spread their empire across the world, conquering country after country, from Syria to Britain. Throughout their conquests, there was no one powerful or strong enough to stop them. That is, except for the Persians.

According to "History Net," as the Roman Empire grew in strength, so did the Persian Empire. This is the reason why the two fought many wars against each other. Their conflict lasted for six centuries with the war beginning around 54 B.C. and ending around A.D. 628. The history between Rome and Persia involves many big and small conflicts and many deaths of great leaders.

During this six-century-long struggle, border towns and provinces were passed back and forth in the Near East. One day, the Romans would have the territory, and then the next day, the Persians would take it back.

Normally, when two empires share such a balance of power, they find a way to coexist. From 31 B.C. to A.D. 14, the Roman Emperor Augustus negotiated peace between the two empires. This peace only lasted for a century, and they were back to war once again. If you look at Rome's history, you can see that, for them, coexistence was not an option.

They went from a small Italian city to an undefeatable empire by conquering and winning wars. It was this dominant trait that stopped the two empires from coexisting and led to the longest war in history.

#52

Spiked Dog Collars Look Cool And Are A Good Defense Against Wolves.

Today, spiked dog collars are used as an accessory to make a dog look cool or menacing. However, when they were first created, they served a much greater purpose.

These spiked collars originated from Turkey, and they were called wolf collars. This is because they were used to protect the wearer from a wolf attack.

According to "The Vintage News," the wolf collars were designed to have chiseled spikes that varied in size but were mostly three inches long.

The design and make of the collar depended on the area it came from.

In some of the poorer areas, it would be made out of wood, and in some of the richer areas, it would be made out of iron. The design also depended on the skill and style of the one who made it.

The collars were given to dogs that were tasked with guarding livestock such as sheep from wolves. Usually, a wolf would go for their victim's throat during a fight, but while the dog was wearing this collar, he would be protected from that. Sheep are usually guarded by multiple dogs with one main leader.

The leader was the one given the honor of wearing the collar, and according to some myths, they were only given the collar after proving themselves worthy of wearing it.

#53
A 15 Year Old Built The World's Largest Grand Piano.

Normally when you think of a grand piano, you think of something big, right? It should be a grand sight to behold. Well, there is no grander sight than the Alexander Piano, which is displayed in the workshop of the one who built it when he was just 15 years old.

At almost 19 feet long, it is the largest grand piano in the world.

According to "Atlas Obscura," Adrian Mann began building the grand piano when he was only 15 years old. He started building the piano back in 2004 after asking his teacher a question about brass strings in instruments that his teacher couldn't answer.

Adrian decided that he would find the answer himself and, in the process, build a grand piano. Building it was a team effort as he was given plenty of help from friends, family, and neighbors.

They provided him with space to build it, donated money, gave him timber, and provided the tools he needed.

He finally finished the piano in 2009 at the age of 20 and named it after his great-great-grandfather.

The Alexander Piano is twice as large as a normal concert grand piano.

It has toured New Zealand, the county in which it was created, and has made many appearances and been played by musicians of every skill.

#54
Your Head Can Increase Signal Range.

It's not unheard of for someone to point their car remote at their head in order to unlock their car. Many people have posted this little myth and videos of it in action. However, is it true?

Does pointing your car's remote at your head actually increase its signal range, and if so, why does it do it? According to "The Naked Scientists," yes it does work and there could be one of two reasons why it works.

When you point your car remote at your head, the cavity that is your head is either acting as a ground plane or a resonator. This is the technical reason as to why it works. Your head is acting as an antenna for the signal and increasing not only its strength but also its range.

The non-technical reason is that you are simply lifting the remote further from the ground when you do this, and that is why the signal is being strengthened. No matter what the reason is, it's a nice trick to try when you get the chance.

#55
There Is Still An Active Volcano In Colorado.

A volcano in Colorado, named Dotsero Crater, is one of the country's only active volcanoes. Although it is still active, it has been called only a moderate threat to human activity in the area by the United States Geological Survey.

According to "9 News," the volcano is not expected to erupt any time soon, despite still being considered active.

A volcano is listed as active by the USGS if it has erupted in the last 10,000 years.

To us, that seems like a long time, but in geologic time, it's actually not very long at all. Dotsero Crater last erupted 4,200 years ago; around that time, the pyramids in Egypt were being built.

This timeline means that this volcano can be listed as still being active, but just because a volcano is listed as active does not mean it is ready to erupt any time soon.

The existence of Dotsero Crater is actually a mystery to geologists. Most of the volcanic activity in this area stopped about 30 million years ago.

Nobody told Dotsero that. The fact that this volcano was able to erupt twice in the past 6,000 years when the rest of the volcanoes are dead is amazing and creates a bit of a mystery.

#56

Apple Paid $1.7 Million For Land That Wasn't Even Worth Half That.

Donnie and Kathy Fulbright lived on their modest property in North Carolina for 34 years. They had no plans of selling or moving. They spent a mere $6,000 on the house which sits on only 1 acre of land, but it was enough for their life. That was until the big company Apple Inc. set its eyes on their small patch of land for their plans known as "Project Dolphin," or the construction of a datacenter.

According to "Mail Online," Apple paid the couple $1.7 million for their property. The couple rejected Apple's first and second offer, but on the third attempt, Apple told them to "put a price on it," and they did.

The couple took the money Apple paid them for their small property and used it to build a 4,200 square-foot dream house that sits on 49 acres of land and comes with a pond and a jacuzzi. They may not have wanted to sell their house of 34 years at first, but now they are living in their dream home.

#57

About 50 Percent Of The World's Gold Comes From South Africa.

A rocky ridge in South Africa, known as Witwatersrand, is considered to be one of the largest and richest gold deposits in the world.

This rich deposit was first discovered in 1886, and since then, over 2 billion ounces of gold have been mined from it.

According to "Atlas Obscura," it's believed that the underground geological formation known as the Witwatersrand Basin used to be the floor of a prehistoric sea.

This is where rivers would have deposited sediments that formed gold and other minerals. It's estimated that about 40 to 50 percent of all the gold mined in the world comes from the Witwatersrand Basin.

The basin stretches in a wide arc that covers 250 miles. It runs from Johannesburg to Welkom.

The discovery of this mined sparked a gold rush in which the city of Johannesburg was created, and within a mere 10 years, it became the largest city in South Africa.

It's said that the mines in the Witwatersrand Basin are some of the deepest mines in the world.

The deepest one, known as Mponeng, extends 2.5 miles below the surface and is home to the world's tallest elevator.

#58

On A Remote Norwegian Island, It Is Illegal To Die.

A small town, named Longyearbyen, is located on an island halfway between the North Pole and mainland Norway. The town has only 2,000 residents at a given time, and they deal with a lot of problems.

During the winter, it stays dark with there being no difference between day and night for three to four months. They share the island with about 1,000 polar bears that cause a constant threat to the townspeople. It's also so cold there that it is illegal to die.

According to "Men's Health," since 1950, people haven't been allowed to die on the island. It is so cold there that the locals realized that the bodies in the cemetery weren't decomposing.

The cold was preserving the bodies so well that in 1998, scientists examined the bodies of victims who had died in 1918 of the flu pandemic and were still able to find live samples of the virus. The locals then became scared that diseases would be able to spread quickly if the bodies that were buried in the cemetery weren't decomposing.

They made it illegal for anyone else to be buried on the island, with the exception of cremation urns being allowed to be buried there.

Few people take up this option, so when they become terminally ill or are believed to be near their time, they are flown to the mainland to spend the rest of their days and eventually die. They are then buried on the mainland or anywhere of their choosing.

You may want to visit this small town for an excellent view of the Northern Lights, just make sure you don't die.

#59
A Coffee Taster Insured His Tongue For 10 Million Euros.

Many stars, athletes, and artists of all kinds have insured parts of their bodies, so insuring body parts shouldn't come as a big shock. But what may be surprising is that someone has insured their tongue. According to "The Telegraph," that person is Gennaro Pelliccia, the taster for the company Costa Coffee who insured his tongue for 10 million euros with Lloyd's of London. Why would someone do that?

Well, Costa Coffee has an annual turnover of 216 million euros or more. Unlike most of today's coffee shops, like Starbucks, they have been doing great. Where Starbucks has been forced to close down over 100 of its stores worldwide, Costa Coffee has said they intend to open up another 100 stores around the world this year.

They are thriving in the coffee industry, maybe because their coffee is priced cheaper than other stores or it just tastes better. The latter is due to the quality control of their taster, the man who insured his tongue. Pelliccia says that his taste buds and sensory skills are crucial to his profession, which is why he didn't hesitate to insure his tongue for such a large sum.

Pelliccia's insurance policy makes his tongue worth more than Bruce Springsteen's voice!

#60

There Is A Version Of Rugby Played Underwater.

Unsurprisingly, this version of rugby that is played underwater is called Underwater Rugby. The game was invented in 1961 in Germany.

It was mainly popular in Nordic countries and was known as UW-Polo or underwater polo. Since the first championship in 1978, the game's rules have changed, and it has evolved into a competitive game popular in over 17 countries.

According to the World Underwater Federation or CMAS, underwater rugby consists of two teams with 15 players each.

There are 12 players in the game at any given time, while three players sit on the side as potential substitutes.

During the game, there are only six players on each team in the pool, while the other six stand on the side of the pool ready to be swapped out at any time.

The game is played in a pool that is between 12 and 22 meters long and between 8 and 12 meters wide. The pool is usually 3.5 or 5 meters deep as well.

The players are wearing fins, a snorkel, and a diving mask. Each game consists of 15-minute halves and a 5-minute half-time break. It's not that different from the actual game of rugby, besides the fact that they're playing in a pool with a plastic ball filled with saltwater.

#61

GPS Is Free, But It Costs $2 Million A Day To Operate.

The Pentagon's Global Positioning System is a free system used around the world so people all over the globe can know where they are and find where they want to go. It has helped all of us avoid scanning street signs and getting lost on a dead-end street while looking for a friend's house. It's really great that this kind of service is free to use, but it's not completely free for the Pentagon to keep it running.

According to "Time," the annual operating cost of the GPS is around $750 million. It is made up of 24 satellites positioned in a very specific constellation around the Earth.

It originally cost the Pentagon $12 billion just to put the satellites into orbit around the Earth. Since then, the GPS has cost the Pentagon approximately $2 million a day to operate, but we don't have to pay a cent. Americans do pay something, however, since their tax money funds it.

#62

Bulls Are Color-Blind, So They Have No Opinion On The Color Red.

For a very long time, people have believed that bulls hate the color red, which is why they charge at that man holding the little red cape during a bullfight. The sport, although unpopular among many, brings to mind that classic image for almost everyone.

The bull charges at the matador who angers him by waving a small red cape about. Although most people believe the reason the bull is angry is because of the red color of the cape, that just isn't the case.

According to "Live Science," most cattle, including bulls, are color-blind, specifically to the color red. Recent research has proven that it is not the red color of the matador's cape that angers the bull, but the movement of it. The matador usually waves the flag around in the arena, and that is what angers the bull, not the color.

On the Discovery Channel in 2007, the MythBusters tested this myth. They placed a live bull in an arena with three flags, one red, one white, and one blue. The bull charged at all three flags regardless of their colors. To further test this, they then placed a man, completely dressed in red, in the arena with the bull.

The man stood completely still while cowboys on horses, not dressed in red, rode around the arena.

The bull charged at each of the cowboys and completely ignored the man dressed in red, which proves that bulls are angered by movement and not by color.

So why is a red cape used in bullfighting if it serves no purpose? The cape does serve a purpose, although it is a more sinister one.

At the end of the show when the Matador pulls out his sword to kill the bull, the red cape is used to hide the blood splatter from the crowd.

#63
Until 2016, You Weren't Allowed To Sing "Happy Birthday" In Public.

Everyone knows the song "Happy Birthday," and we've all sung it once or twice around a candlelit cake.

We've also all sat there awkwardly as it was sung to us. However, up until recently, the song was copyrighted. That means that you couldn't sing the song in public without having to pay royalties to the people who owned it.

According to "ARS Technica," a lawsuit that was filed in 2013 and settled in 2016 challenged the song's copyright. "Happy Birthday" shares the same melody as a 19th-century children's song called "Good Morning to You." It's alleged that that same author of the "Good Morning" song, Patty Hill, changed the lyrics to the song in order to create the "Happy Birthday" song.

However, the judge added that in his view, it is questionable whether or not Patty Hill is the actual author of the song. Music publisher Warner/Chappell claims that the song was copyrighted since 1935, and they have been profiting from it ever since, making about $2 million annually from royalties on the song.

#64
How Much Wood Would A Woodchuck Chuck?

How much wood would a woodchuck chuck if a woodchuck could chuck wood? Phew! Try saying that five times fast. It's a famous tongue twister that many have been using to have a laugh and challenge each other with for ages.

But could it be more than a fun little tongue twister? Some people have taken this tongue twister and seen it as an actual question, and they've gone on a search for answers.

According to the American Forest Foundation, Richard Thomas, a wildlife technician, did some calculations and was able to answer the question.

A woodchuck, also known as a groundhog, burrows into the ground and chucks dirt out of the hole. We know that a woodchuck can chuck about 35-cubic feet of dirt while it is digging out its burrow.

Thomas figured that if a woodchuck could chuck wood, then it would chuck enough wood to equal the amount of dirt it does chuck. That would be 700 pounds of wood. If a woodchuck could and wanted to chuck wood, then it would chuck about 700 pounds of wood.

This is, of course, depending on several factors: the size of the woodchuck, the woodchuck's desire to chuck wood, and its need to chuck wood.

Taking these factors into account, it would be a little more or a little less than 700 pounds of wood.

#65

During WWII, The Japanese Mistook Potatoes For Grenades.

The USS *O'Bannon* was one of the most decorated ships during WWII. It was named after First Lieutenant Presley Neville O'Bannon, who was considered to be a hero during the Barbary War and went on to become a U.S. Marine Corps legend.

The USS *O'Bannon* was just as incredible as the man it was named after. It could travel at 35 knots and was equipped with torpedo tubes, over 140 guns, and six depth charge tracks, but these were not the star weapons in 1944 when it battled against a Japanese submarine.

According to "War History Online," the *O'Bannon* encountered an RO-34, which was a Kaichu VI-type submarine. It was medium-sized and equipped with both an anti-aircraft machine gun and anti-aircraft gun.

The submarine was surfaced on the South Pacific at night in 1944 when the *O'Bannon* spotted it. The initial plan was for the *O'Bannon* to ram the sub, but as the ship approached the sub at incredible speed, the crew realized that the sub might have a minelayer. If they collided with the Japanese, it would mean disaster for both the Americans and the Japanese. Moments before impact, the *O'Bannon* veered out of the way in order to avoid the collision.

Now the *O'Bannon* was positioned too close to the submarine to be able to fire its many guns at it. The Japanese submarine, however, was in the perfect position to fire at them. With no other option on hand, the crew of the *O'Bannon* did the only thing they could think of. They started throwing potatoes at the submarine. The Japanese didn't know what to think of this, and in the mindset of war, they mistook the potatoes as hand grenades. This started a panic among the Japanese.

They started throwing the potatoes back at the *O'Bannon* and tossing them into the sea as quickly as they could. They did this instead of opening fire on the ship.

This gave the *O'Bannon* enough time to maneuver far enough away from the submarine so they could begin firing. They sank the Japanese submarine and won the battle.

#66

The Oldest Bottle Of Wine Is 1,650 Years Old.

Wine has been a part of human history for a very long time. It's thought that the first bottles of wine date back farther than written history itself. According to one theory, we can date the making and drinking of wine as far back as 10000 to 8000 B.C. This is because people were starting to settle down in permanent homes.

When people started settling down in places instead of moving around, they were able to grow crops and turn those crops into wine. However, this is just a theory, and we don't have any bottles of wine from this period, but we do have a bottle of wine that is older than anyone living on Earth today.

According to "My Modern Met," the oldest bottle of wine in existence is 1,650 years old. This wine was made and bottled in the 4th century between A.D. 325 and 359. It is known as the Speyer Wine Bottle after the name of the area it was found in, a Roman nobleman's tomb during an excavation of the tomb in Germany.

Nobody knows what this wine smells or tastes like. Scientists are unsure of what would happen to the liquid in the bottle if it were exposed to air. They decided to protect the wine in the bottle for historical purposes and keep it sealed with a thick wax stopper and some olive oil.

The bottle is now being displayed at the Historical Museum of Palatinate in Germany. Rumor says that only one man has held the bottle because everyone else is too scared to try.

#67
Free Wi-Fi As Homage To Nikola Tesla's Vision.

Nikola Tesla was a great inventor and a fantastic visionary. He worked for the people and believed in free and safe electricity for the world and free wireless communication.

Tesla was not given the respect he deserved when he was alive, but today, people who admire his vision are showing him that respect.

In Silicon Valley, you will find a great statue of Nikola Tesla, sculpted by Terry Guyer, standing tall and proud. According to "Tesla Universe," the idea to build the statue was thought up by Northern Imagination, a holding company in California. They were backed by 722 people on their Kickstarter.

The plans began on June 2, 2013, and the statue was unveiled to the public on December 7, 2013. The statue provides that area with a free Wi-Fi signal as an homage to Tesla's vision of free wireless communication. The statue also guards a time capsule that is to be opened on January 7, 2043. I can't wait to see what's in it!

#68
Only Official Members Of Native American Tribes Can Possess An Eagle Feather.

Eagles are among the many protected birds in America. Not only are they an American symbol, but they are also endangered. It's no surprise then that killing a bald eagle is illegal and comes with hefty fines and jail time, even if it was an accident.

According to the Association on American Indian Affairs, even possessing an eagle's feather is against the law, unless you're part of a federally recognized Native American tribe.

Some Native American tribes use eagle feathers in religious rituals and for other cultural purposes. The law in America allows for Native American tribes that have been federally recognized by the government to legally possess the feathers of an eagle.

For those that aren't part of a tribe, they can't even pick an eagle's feather up off the ground without breaking the law.

Of course, this law only allows these tribes to possess the feathers that they have been given by other tribes or have found on the ground. They aren't allowed to harm an eagle in any way in order to get the feathers.

If you find an eagle's feather lying on the ground, just leave it alone, unless you're part of a federally recognized tribe that is.

#69
This Type Of Fish Communicates Through Flatulence.

Animals communicate in different ways. Just look at humans. We are able to speak with each other and perfectly understand what we are saying. However, other animals won't be able to understand us or speak to us.

All animals communicate with others in their own way. One of the more interesting methods of communication is seen in the red herring fish.

According to the American Association for the Advancement of Science, red herring fish communicate with each other using flatulence.

Recent research done by Magnus Wahlberg and his colleagues found that red herrings make noises by squeezing air bubbles out of their backsides.

Red herrings, unlike other fish, have very good hearing. It would make sense that they are making these sounds purposefully to communicate with each other.

A previous study showed that these fish would often release bubbles from their backsides when they were scared.

Ben Wilson from Simon Fraser University furthered the research by putting some herrings in tanks and recording them. He noticed many things, including the fact that the herrings made a distinctive flatulence noise when it got dark and all the fish gathered together.

This proved that they were using the flatulence to communicate in some way. Fish are really weird.

#70

China Is Building Panda-Shaped Solar Farms.

In China, renewable energy isn't a big thing. It's needed, but not enough young minds are interested in it for it to make a difference. In 2015, a young girl came up with a plan that she hoped would get more young people interested in renewable energy. Turns out it was a good idea.

According to "Business Insider," Ada Li Yan-tung was only 15 years old when she presented her idea to get young minds more interested in renewable energy at the United Nations Youth climate conference in 2015.

Yan-tung suggested that building panda-shaped solar farms would be a good way to get young minds more interested in renewable energy.

The United Nations Development Program and Panda Green Energy Group worked with her a year later in order to bring her vision to life.

By 2017, the first panda-shaped solar farm was built. It takes up 248 acres and resembles two smiling pandas from above.

This solar farm, which was built in Datong, was connected to the electricity grid in the month of June

2017, and it is capable of powering over 10,000 homes a year.

After the success of the first solar power plant in Datong, they now plan to build 99 more across China. This project is going to cost them $3 billion in investment, but you could say that it is worth it.

#71

Some People Were Forced To Watch Paint Dry For 10 Hours.

People in the U.K. take their films very seriously, and they are very strict when it comes to censoring their films. The BBFC, or British Board of Film Classification, holds a place of great importance in the movie industry in the U.K. A film won't be shown in the U.K. until it has received a certification from the BBFC.

This is similar to the PG, R, and other ratings that are given to movies in the U.S. by the Motion Picture Association of America.

The worst part about this system is that the BBFC is very picky, and it charges roughly £1,000 ($1,425) to review a feature-length film. There is no chance for your film to be shown in the U.K. until it is reviewed by the BBFC, and that is a steep price to pay for the process.

Members of the BBFC have to sit through an entire film before they are allowed to give it their review, and that is why filmmaker Charlie Lyne came up with his brilliant idea.

According to "Quartz," Charlie Lyn sent the BBFC a

10-hour long documentary called "Paint Drying" in order to protest the system. The documentary was literally 10 hours watching a wall of white paint drying.

The film was publicly funded and filmed by Charlie. He sent it into the BBFC, whose members were forced to watch the entirety of the 10-hour long film before giving their rating.

They did give it a rating. The documentary "Paint Drying" is suitable for viewers who are aged 4 or older.

#72

Half Of The Apartments In Los Angeles Don't Have Fridges.

When you're looking at an apartment to rent, the one thing you don't normally look out for is if the apartment has a fridge. It's normal to think that any apartment you want to rent would come with a fridge.

You'd expect an apartment to have a fridge just as much as you'd expect it to have a toilet. However, if you're looking for an apartment in Los Angeles, you may need to rent a fridge as well.

According to "LA Weekly," it's common to find an apartment for rent in Los Angeles that doesn't come with a fridge. In fact, it's been reported that about half of the apartments for rent don't come with fridges.

This might be hard to believe, but the fact that the owners of these apartments don't have to provide their renters with a fridge is completely legal.

If you ask the Housing and Community Investment Department, they will tell you that a fridge is considered an amenity.

This means that the landlord is not required to provide one. An amenity is considered unnecessary like a garage unit or air-conditioning. Most people would argue that a fridge is a necessity and not an amenity, but that's not the case in Los Angeles.

If you're planning on moving to Los Angeles, I would suggest bringing your own fridge.

#73

If You Work At This Company, You Can Call In Hungover.

We've all done it once or twice before. We had a big night and woke up feeling dusty the next morning and realized that we actually have to go to work.

We can't tell our boss that we're hungover from partying the night before, so we do the only thing we can do.

We lie and say we're sick. We call our boss, fake a few coughs, and make it sound like we're too sick to even talk, and they end up giving us an off day. According to "10 daily," if you work for this company in the U.K., you won't have to do that anymore.

This company in the U.K. is a digital marketing company called Audit Lab, and it has a hangover policy.

If you wake up with a hangover, all you have to do is call your boss and tell them that, and they'll allow you to work from home that day. However, employees are only allowed a certain number of hangover days. This stops them from taking too many when they don't need to.

The company said that they did it because they

wanted to be able to offer something to the younger generation who goes out and parties most nights. Since they are a digital marketing company, most of their talented workers are young millennials, and they knew that would be the case.

According to them, no one overuses or misuses the hangover policy, which is a miracle in itself.

#74

There's A Russian Village Filled With Tightrope Walkers.

In Russia, you will find a small village hidden in the hills of the Greater Causcus Mountains called Tsovkra-1. In this tiny, secluded village, there is a tightrope-walking tradition that everyone upholds, if they can.

According to "Smithsonian Magazine," tightrope walking has been a tradition in this town for so long that nobody in the town even remembers how or why the tradition was started. All they know is that they must keep the tradition alive.

Men and women, old and young, practice tightrope walking in all kinds of weather, and the village children reportedly study it in school. Now, there are fewer than 400 people living in the small town, but everyone who is physically able to keeps up the tradition.

The small town, which is accompanied by a numeral to help set it apart from a nearby village with the same name, produced 17 women and men who became famous Soviet Union tightrope walkers in circuses.

Although no one knows for sure how the tradition started, there are a few rumors. One is of romance; it's thought that the men of the village grew tired of trekking through the valley to their neighboring village to court women, so they developed a short cut.

They strung up a rope that stretched from one side of the valley to the other and used it to crawl across. The braver men began walking across the rope to impress the women; eventually, it became a test of manhood, and later on, a cherished tradition.

#75

Domino's Pizza Delivers Via Reindeer In Japan.

Domino's Pizza in Japan is currently training reindeer to deliver their pizzas in the winter. They released a video to the public of their employees leading a reindeer around a parking-lot with pizza boxes on its back. The staff even have an app on their smartphones to monitor the reindeer's progress, which shows the animal's face on a map as it moves around.

According to "CNBC," Domino's Japan is working on a variety of delivery methods with the reindeer just being a small part of it.

They do plan on rolling out the reindeer delivery system soon, although at the moment, the reindeer are dropping the pizza boxes on the floor and the employees are running just to keep up with them.

We may see reindeer delivering pizzas come next winter, but who knows.

#76

The Happiest Countries In The World Consume A Lot Of Antidepressants.

Where you're from in the world definitely impacts how happy you are. If you pull up a list of the happiest countries in the world, you'll find that most of them are located in Scandinavia.

Scandinavia is a dark and cold place, one of the darkest and coldest on Earth, and yet everyone there seems to be so happy. It does seem suspicious that people living in such conditions could really be so happy about it.

According to "Opposing Views," there may be something else at work that is making these people seem happier than they actually are.

New reports from the Organization for Economic Co-operation and Development show a link between the happiest countries on Earth and the consumption of antidepressants. The research shows the number of antidepressants that are consumed on average per person in these countries.

According to the research, Iceland, which is near Scandinavia, ranks highest. There are 101 daily doses of antidepressants per 1,000 people there.

Denmark is next, followed by Portugal, then Sweden, and Finland. Norway ranks ninth on the list.

All of these places are high on the list of the happiest countries in the world, and they are also high on the list of consumption of antidepressants.

Can they really be called the happiest countries in the world when they are taking so many antidepressants?

A Non-Violent Escape From Prison In Mexico Won't Be Punished.

The need and want for freedom is considered a basic human right in Mexico, and that's why escaping from prison is not a crime. According to "Digg.com," you can escape prison in Mexico and not face any kind of punishment, provided that you complied with the few terms and conditions.

In this country, the law recognizes that the want for freedom is a basic human right, so they will not punish you for going after that freedom, but if you break any laws in your pursuit of that freedom, then they can punish you.

For example, if you break a window and jump out of it, you have damaged property, and they can punish you for that.

In a more extreme case, if you harm another prisoner or guard during your escape, then you can be punished for that. An escape from prison can't be punished, but a violent escape can add six months to three years to your current prison time.

There are a few other conditions if you do escape from prison. The time you are spending outside the prison doesn't count toward the jail time you have to serve. Therefore, if you are ever caught after you escape, you will have to serve the rest of the sentence that you had left when you escaped.

Also, if you are captured again, you can no longer be considered a good conduct prisoner. Sometimes good conduct prisoners are given reduced sentences, but if you have escaped from prison and been recaptured, you won't receive this luxury.

Mexico isn't the only country that does it. The same or similar laws can be found in Germany and Australia.

Starfish Don't Have Blood!

Starfish, which are also known as sea stars, are surrounded by incredible and unknown facts. They are one of the most recognizable fish in the ocean, but did you know that they aren't even considered to be fish?

According to "WorldStrides," starfish don't have blood vessels in their body. If you cut them, they won't bleed because they don't have any blood. The starfish have a water vascular system instead. Seawater is pumped throughout their bodies using the tube feet that are situated on the underside of their body. The water vascular system uses the tube feet to pump seawater through the starfish's body much like a heart would pump blood throughout our body.

A starfish is also able to drop one of its limbs the same way a lizard would drop its tail. If a starfish is attacked, it will forfeit one of its arms to the predator. While the predator is busy with the starfish's arm, the starfish can escape the attack and survive another day. This is okay because, much like a lizard, the starfish can grow a new arm, but the arm will take up to a year to fully grow back.

#79
The Bees Knees Isn't Just An Expression.

You've most likely heard someone say the expression "the bee's knees" before. But do you know why people use that expression and where it actually comes from? Well, it's probably because a bee does actually have knees, and the expression is derived from what a bee's knees look like. The "bee's knees" means something sweet and good or something that is at the height of excellence. It might be said like this: "Oh, you got me a cup of coffee; you're the bee's knees." The expression probably came from the sight of an actual bee's knees.

According to "The Naked Scientists," bees have segmented legs just like us. The joint that connects these segments can be considered their knees. When bees fly around from flower to flower collecting pollen, they tend to store some of this pollen in the hairy baskets on their knees. They have baskets filled with hairs on their knees, and the pollen sticks to this easily. This may be where the expression comes from, because when a bee's knees are covered in pollen, they are good and sweet and a spectacular sight to behold.

#80

When You Exercise, The Fat You Lose Is Exhaled Out Of Your Body.

In this modern society, most people are obsessed with dieting, weight-loss, and reaching that elusive size zero dress. However, in a world so obsessed with losing weight, does anyone actually know where the fat goes when we lose it? According to "Science Alert," we breathe it out.

Up until recently, it was believed that when we exercise, we convert the fat into heat and energy. However, if this were true, it would go against the Law of Conservation of Mass. New studies have revealed the truth of where our fat goes when we exercise.

A physicist and T.V. presenter, Ruben Meerman, was able to do some research in order to find out the truth about fat conversion. When we put on weight, it is because the excess proteins and carbohydrates we have eaten are converted to something called triglycerides, and then those are stored inside our body's fat cells. In order to lose weight, you need to break down the triglycerides so you can access the carbon inside them.

Meerman was able to determine that oxygen atoms

are shared between the hydrogen and carbon you find in fat. The ratio was 2:1, and this forms carbon dioxide and water.

This means that when we exercise, we break down the carbon in the fat cells into carbon dioxide and water using the oxygen atoms that we breathe in. He was then able to determine that we breathe out about 84 percent of the fat molecules, and 16 percent is turned into water that we pee out.

Just breathing won't help you to lose weight, though. You need to use exercise to break down the fat molecules first, then you can exhale them.

#81

Cats Only Meow At Humans, Not Other Cats, As A Way To Communicate.

A cat's meow is distinguishable from every other sound in the world. It's so cute that it's impossible to ignore a cat that meows at you. A cat's meow is a simple noise, but they use it to communicate many different things.

They use it to tell us that they want something; they use it to warn us that something is wrong, and they use it simply to say hello. Would it shock you to know that cats only meow at humans?

According to the American Society for the Prevention of Cruelty to Animals, adult cats don't meow at other cats at all. They only meow at humans. Kittens are known to meow at the mothers in order to communicate if they are hungry, cold, or hurt. However, after kittens grow old enough, they no longer meow at other cats, including their mothers. A cat will stop meowing at other cats when it gets older, but they will continue meowing at humans for the rest of their lives.

Cats also have three different forms of communication. While cats don't meow at other cats, they do yowl at other cats. Yowling is like meowing, but it is louder and more drawn out. A cat will do this during the breeding season to attract other cats.

A different form of yowling is also used when cats are in a standoff with each other and they are trying to warn the other not to fight them. The other form of communication comes as a hiss, which is a cat's way of saying, "Back off, I'm not in the mood."

#82

Video Games Are More Effective At Battling Depression Than Other Methods.

If someone asks you what the opposite of play or fun is, what would you say? You and most other people would probably answer with "work" or "boring," but there is another answer to both of those questions. Brian Sutton-Smith, a psychologist of play, first offered the idea that the opposite of play or fun is depression.

According to "Slate Technology," Sutton-Smith, who rose to prominence in the 1950s and 60s, was able to observe that in most people when they are playing, they experience more self-confidence, positive emotions, physical energy, excitement, and curiosity.

This is the complete opposite of the actions and feelings of people who are clinically depressed. Sutton-Smith was able to figure all this out before the technology and science we have today that helps scientists study brain waves and blood flow patterns. What he observed was right.

Recently, scientists were able to study gamers as they were playing their video games. The results? When we play video games, two parts of our brain are activated, the region associated with goal-orientation and motivation, also known as the reward pathway, and the region associated with memory and learning. When we play a game, we are always focused on a goal, and this gives us motivation and a sense of self-confidence.

We start to think of our ability to succeed in reaching this goal, and the reward we will get when we do.

The two regions of the brain that are stimulated when you are playing games are usually under-stimulated when you are depressed. Playing games could help stimulate these areas of the brain and combat depression.

#83
You Can Get An Insurance Policy Against Alien Abduction.

Insurance is a big thing, and these days you can get insurance for almost anything. You can even insure parts of your body, like most movie stars, athletes, and artists do. There are certain insurance policies that you should absolutely have, and then there are some insurance policies that you probably didn't know existed.

According to "The Balance," you can take out an insurance policy against alien abduction. Alien Abduction Insurance (AAI), which is also known as UFO insurance, covers you in the event that you are abducted by non-human life forms, which are also known as aliens. Your insurance will be paid out if the terms and conditions of the policy are met and there is substantial proof. Different insurance companies are taking different approaches to UFO insurance. Some who offer the insurance offer it as more of a gimmick that you can give as a gift to a friend. Others are taking it very seriously, and some companies have actually paid some claims.

#84
The Theft Of The Mona Lisa Made The Painting Famous.

Today, everyone in the world knows and can recognize the famous smile of Leonardo da Vinci's Mona Lisa. She is one of the most famous paintings in the world. But why is she famous? Is it because she is a wonderful work of art by a very talented artist? Is it because of that memorable smile? Is it because it is a painting of a mystery woman who no one knows the true name of?

It could be all of these reasons or it could be an entirely different reason altogether.

According to "CNN World," the reason for the Mona Lisa's popularity might be because of her theft over a hundred years ago.

In August 1911, the Mona Lisa was taken right off of the walls of the Louvre in Paris by the handyman Vincenzo Peruggia.

During the search for the painting that lasted 2 years, the painting was shown in numerous international newspapers, and before long, everyone knew the face of Mona Lisa.

The theft of the Mona Lisa drew more visitors to the

empty space where she used to sit than when she was actually at the Louvre.

Now the Mona Lisa is the crown jewel of the Louvre, and she is famous throughout the world.

However, there are some that think that if the handyman had snuck another painting out of the Louvre, it would be a completely different story.

#85

Over A Million People Live In Nuclear Bunkers In Beijing.

I bet you didn't know that between 100,000 and 1 million people live in underground bomb shelters in Beijing. The origin of these bomb shelters dates back to 1969. There was a lot of tension between the Soviet Union and China back then.

That year, Soviet border guards were ambushed by Chinese troops at Zhenbao Island, which, at the time, was a disputed territory in the middle of the Ussuri River. The Ussuri River separated Russia's Far East from northeastern China, so you can imagine how the dispute became bloody quickly. This was known as the other Cold War.

Chairman Mao Zedong in China advised the cities to prepare for nuclear fallout by building bomb shelters capable of withstanding the impact of a nuclear bomb.

According to "National Geographic," over 10,000 of these nuclear bunkers were constructed in Beijing alone. When the Cold War ended and China opened its borders, there was no longer a need for these bunkers. In the early 1980s, the defense department leased the bunkers to landlords who then turned the small nuclear shelters into very small residential apartments. Now, more than a million people live in these bunkers that are situated underneath the streets of Beijing.

The living conditions in these bunkers are extremely harsh and even illegal. They have plumbing and a proper sewage system, and even electricity, but the air down there is stale and moldy. It's very easy to catch a disease down there, and the bathrooms and kitchen areas that the residents have to share are cramped and unsanitary.

Still, people chose to live down there because it's cheap and they have no other option. At least they'll be safe if there ever is a nuclear fallout.

#86

A Guide Dog Saved Her Owner From 9/11.

No one is soon to forget the tragic events that took place on September 11, 2001. It was a horrible day that scarred the nation. A lot of people died, and many more were injured and left traumatized for life.

One man managed to escape the horror just moments before one of the buildings came falling down, thanks in large part to his guide dog.

According to "People Magazine," Michael Hingson was saved that day by his yellow Labrador guide dog, Roselle. He was sitting at his desk getting ready for the busy day ahead when the American Airlines jet hit the upper floor of the building.

There were fumes from the jet's engines flowing into the building and the stairwell. With the help of Roselle, Michael and a few of his co-workers rushed to the stairwell and began the long trek to the ground.

With the fumes surrounding them, the pair walked slowly and calmly down the 78 flights of stairs. Michael says that it was a team effort.

"She kept me as calm as I kept her," Michael said. Roselle showed her true strength and resilience that day as the two reached the ground only minutes before the second tower collapsed.

The two of them scrambled to get out of the area as it was filled with noxious dust. To this day, Michael says that he learned one thing from Roselle that day, and it was the importance of teamwork and trust.

Roselle, unfortunately, died at the age of 13 in 2011 from an auto-immune disorder. She was surrounded by Michael and the people who loved her.

#87

The True Origins Of The Thumbs-Up Sign.

If you think about the thumbs-up sign, you probably think of what it means or the emoji that resembles it. How many of us have actually thought about its origins?

You probably think you know where it came from, but if you're going to say ancient gladiators in Rome, then you're wrong. Most think that the origin of the thumbs-up and thumbs-down gestures come from the Roman emperors deciding whether or not a gladiator was killed.

According to "Portable Press," this simply isn't true. The emperors never decided if a gladiator was killed or not, and the gladiators were sentenced to death most of the time anyway. The true origins of the thumbs-up gesture can most likely be linked to WWII.

In WWII, the Flying Tiger Brigade was made up of American pilots, and they were based in China. The locals in the area would show their support for the pilots by giving them a thumbs-up. The thumbs-up is a Chinese gesture that literally means "number one" and figuratively means "nice job." Then the pilots throughout the U.S. and the Allied military adopted the signal and used it to signal that they were "ready to go." This was a visual gesture to the ground crew by the planes who would not be able to hear the pilots over the engines. The signal helped let the ground crew know that the pilot was ready to take off.

The meaning of the thumbs-up gesture has changed a lot since then. Now it means "I approve" or "hello" or "that was a good move." In some places like South America and West Africa, a thumbs-up is an insult and can be translated into "up yours."

#88
The Paint On The Eiffel Tower Weighs The Same As 10 Elephants.

The Eiffel Tower is a symbol that is recognized around the world. It is a great monument that symbolizes the excellence of human craftsmanship.

This kind of symbol requires a lot of work to ensure its longevity.

According to "The Official Eiffel Tower Website," the amount of paint that is used to repaint the Eiffel Tower has a weight equivalent to the weight of 10 elephants.

All the paint used equals 60 tons. The Eiffel Tower itself is made out of puddle iron, which is said to be a practically indestructible metal that can last forever. However, the tower is further protected from oxidation by many coats of paint.

The Eiffel Tower's paint is stripped and reapplied every seven years. It's changed its color throughout the years before we got to the bronze color that we see on it today.

The Eiffel Tower is painted by hand by 25 painters. They strip the paint, clean the metal, apply rust-proofing to it, and then they paint the whole 300-

meter tall tower by hand.

These painters use traditional methods using ropes and harnesses. The process takes up to 18 months to complete, and the tower is not closed down to the public during that time. It costs around 4 million euros every time they have to do this.

#89

When Dinosaurs Roamed The Earth, They Roamed Everywhere.

Humans are spread out all over the Earth today, but even now, there are still some parts of the world that are left uninhabited.

This is because the conditions in these places are so harsh that it isn't possible for humans to exist there. These kinds of conditions didn't seem to bother the dinosaurs when they were still roaming the Earth.

During the period the dinosaurs ruled the earth, which was about 165 million years in total, all the continents on the earth were fused together to form a supercontinent. This supercontinent is known as Pangea. The dinosaurs lived on every part of this supercontinent.

According to the United States Geological Survey, the supercontinent known as Pangea slowly broke apart. The pieces then slowly floated away from each other with dinosaurs still living on each piece.

It took a lot of time, but eventually, the pieces of Pangea floated into the places they are in today. This process is called plate tectonics.

When this happened, dinosaurs were still thriving on

each continent as they split apart and moved into an arrangement that is nearer to the one they are in now.

Dinosaurs were even living in Antarctica at the time, which is a place humans are incapable of living in.

#90

The Quietest Place In The World Isn't Where You'd Expect.

According to "Atlas Obscura," the quietest place in the whole world is the acoustics and architecture test facility at the Orfield Laboratories in Minnesota. This room is recognized by the Guinness Book of Records as the quietest room in the world. Inside the room, the floor is made of mesh and the walls are covered with fiberglass acoustic wedges that are three feet thick.

The room is encased in double walls made of concrete that is a foot thick and steel, and the whole room is closed off by two heavy vault doors. It is known as the anechoic chamber, which means "echo-free."

When the doors are closed and the lights are turned off, the noise levels inside the chamber measure at -9 decibels. If you're unsure how quiet that is, quiet libraries usually measure at 30 decibels.

Steve Orfield, the owner of Orfield Labs, says he likes to challenge people to stay inside the chamber for as long as they can. When the noise levels in an area are that low, your attention and senses are usually turned toward your own body. Eventually, you'll start to notice all the small sounds your body makes. Your stomach gurgling, your nose whistling as you breathe, and your heart pumping in your ears. All these sounds will seem 10 times louder than normal.

Most people struggle to stay in the chamber for more than 20 minutes, and when they leave, they are unsettled and disorientated.

The chamber is actually used as a test room. They test the volume of the sounds that the switches and components on their products make so they can finetune them to be as silent as possible.

#91

The Russians Were 12 Days Late For The 1908 Olympics.

In 1908, the Olympics were being held in London, and according to "Today I Found Out," the Russians arrived 12 days late. The reason the Russians arrived so late was that, at the time, they were still using the Julian calendar while most of the world was using the Gregorian calendar instead. Why did this make them late?

The Gregorian calendar was established by Pope Gregory XIII so it could compensate for the errors in keeping time that had built up over the past centuries.

In the 1500s, Scotland and most Roman Catholic countries started using this calendar.

However, a lot of protestant countries stuck to using the old Julian calendar, which was filled with many errors, for over 200 years.

England was still using the Julian calendar, but they switched to the Gregorian calendar in 1751. Russia, which was a more orthodox country, stuck to the Julian calendar until after the Russian Revolution.

The Russian Revolution took place in 1917, and only after that did the Russians finally make the switch to the Gregorian calendar.

However, they made the switch a bit too late. They were still using the Julian calendar in 1908 during the Olympics, which is the reason why they showed up 12 days late for it.

You would think an embarrassment like that would urge them to make the switch sooner.

#92
The British Pound Is Over 1,200 Years Old.

The British Pound is the oldest currency in the world. According to "CMC Markets," it's about 1,200 years old, with the first version—sterling silver pennies—established in A.D. 775. Since then, the currency has undergone numerous changes.

The Bank of England was established in 1694, and the very first printing of pound banknotes started in 1853. Back then, the notes were only partially printed. The notes were printed with the pound sign and the first digit. The bank had to hand paint the numbers onto the notes and then the note needed to be signed by one of the cashiers. This process seems so complicated they should have just stuck to using coins.

Coins were still popular and kept in circulation. The rarest British coin is the 1933 penny. Apparently, only seven pennies were made that year because there were already so many pennies in circulation. Today, the British Pound is the fourth most traded currency in the market.

93

How Much Horsepower Does A Horse Have?

It may seem like a question no one is going to ask, but if you don't ask, then how will you know that answer? I bet you think one horse probably only has one horsepower. That makes sense, but it's not correct. According to "Energy Education," one horse has the equivalent to 15 horsepower.

Humans are capable of a maximum output of a little more than one horsepower. Tour de France riders can max out 1.2 horsepower over the course of around 15 seconds.

Horsepower is a unit of energy. Power is the term used to describe how fast energy is exchanged. Basically, power is the use of energy divided by how long it takes to use that energy.

Horsepower is the term used to refer to the sustained output of energy from an engine. James Watt was the one who invented the term horsepower, and he helped make great improvements to the steam engine.

The term may seem strange and misleading, but Watt had good reasons when he invented it. He had just finished his steam engine, and he wanted an easy way to show people how good it was. He couldn't say it had the same power as a horse since people already had horses, so what was the point. He instead told them that his engine had the power of 10 horses or 10 horsepower. This instantly made people interested in his engine.

Watt was not lying. The maximum output of a horse is around 15 horsepower, but a horse won't be able to keep up that amount of energy for an entire day.

Watt's engine was able to keep up the 10-horsepower energy throughout the day. Where a horse would get tired and lose energy, the engine would not.

#94

A Blue Whale's Heart Is The Size Of A Car.

A blue whale is an impressive animal in terms of size and beauty. Blue whales are the largest animals on the planet; they're even larger than most dinosaurs were. Every part of a blue whale is large, including its heart.

According to "Whale Facts," the largest of the blue whales was over 100 feet long facts weighed more than 180 tons. However, most blue whales grow to be 70 to 90 feet long and, at most, will weigh between 100 and 150 tons. Such large animals need large arteries in order to pump the blood through the heart, around the large body, and to all the vital organs. Their arteries are so large that a fully grown human could swim through them, if they wanted to, that is.

The heart of a blue whale is also quite large. It can be compared to the size of a small car, like a VW Beetle, and it weighs around 1,300 pounds.

Although the heart weighs so much to us, it's only about 1 percent of the whale's overall weight. The blue whale's heartbeat is so loud, it can be heard from 2 miles away, and it only beats at a rate of 8-10 beats a minute. For comparison, a human heart beats at around 60-80 beats per minute.

#95

The Military Uses Silly String To Detect Trip Wires.

War is a serious thing, and it's not to be made light of at all, but some may laugh when they hear that silly string is playing an important part in the movement of the U.S. military in Iraq.

According to "CBS News," Marcelle Shriver heard about American troops using the silly string to detect trip wires from her son who was a soldier in Iraq. Before entering a building, soldiers would squirt some of the silly string through the door.

The strands can shoot about 10 to 12 feet across a room. If the silly string falls to the ground, then they know that the room is clear, but if it hangs in the air then they might have found a trip wire.

Trip wires are practically invisible otherwise and are high on the list of dangers that American troops face.

Thankfully, silly string is easy to see, can cover a large area if squirted right, and is very light so it won't set off a trip wire by landing on it.

When Shriver heard about this, she started a drive to collect cans of silly string to send to the soldiers in Iraq.

She has collected over 1,000 cans of neon silly string thanks to many donations, including one from Just for Kicks Inc., the creators of the silly string brand.

#96

The U.S. Military Is Using This Snail Shell Design For Military Armor.

A new snail was first discovered in 2003 and has drawn the attention of scientists and military men alike. The snail, which is known as "scaly foot," was discovered living in some of the harshest conditions in the Indian Ocean. According to "CBS News," the next generation of bulletproof vests is going to be modeled off the design of this snail's shell.

The snail lives in areas where there are hydrothermal vents. These vents spew out hot water, and because of this, the snail is exposed to high acidity as well as extreme fluctuations in temperature. The snail also has to deal with predators like crabs. This snail is able to survive these harsh conditions because of the makeup of its three-layered shell.

The first layer, or outer layer, is made of iron sulfides. The middle layer is made up of organic material, and it is much thicker than the other two layers. Scientists liken this layer to a thin protein coating known as the periostracum. The inner layer is composed of aragonite, which is a calcium mineral that is often found in corals. The "scaly foot" is the only known animal species that has iron sulfides as part of its structure.

The way the shell works is by fending off attacks from crabs using the outer layer of the shell. Crabs grab snails with their claws and squeeze them tight. If a crab does this to this snail, the outer layer is designed to crack in a way that keeps the snail inside safe. The shell's cracks fan out along the shell in what is called "microcracking."

They absorb all of the energy from the force of the crab's claws, and they prevent any larger cracks from forming. The iron sulfides can also blunt and damage the claws of the snail's attackers.

This flawless design could be perfect for military armor in the future.

#97
Polar Bears Hunt Walruses By Not Directly Attacking Them.

Polar bears and walruses have shared the same living and hunting grounds for thousands of years. They are both big, strong, and ruthless opponents. However, up until recently, it was unclear whether or not a polar bear would hunt and attack a walrus at all. The recent global changes and melting ice have forced the polar bears and walruses closer together, which has made it easier for scientists to observe their relationship.

A polar bear, especially a young and inexperienced one, will never directly attack a walrus. Walruses are strong and fierce. If a polar bear were to attack one, then it would be in for quite a fight. Their attack method, according to the Russian Geographical Society, is to charge at a group of them.

The hunt would begin with a polar bear walking up to a rockery of resting walruses. Walruses usually sit on the rocky shore in a large group. The polar bear would slowly approach the rockery and then suddenly break out into a run. As the polar bear or bears charge at the walruses, panic will begin. In the panic, the walruses will flee for the safety of the water. While the walruses flee, the polar bears will continue to charge after them, but they won't attack; they simply make sure that the walruses have no space to stop or rest.

This strategy will reveal the youngest and weakest of the walruses. The weak and young will slow down and get separated from the group. These are the walruses that the polar bears eventually attack.

Sometimes a walrus will also be trampled and injured during the panic, which will make them an easy target for the polar bears.

This seems to be the main way that polar bears hunt walruses. Larger and more experienced polar bears will attack a walrus, but they will often leave the fight with some bloody tusk wounds.

It's usually only the male polar bears that will attack a walrus straight on, as female polar bears tend to be more cautious.

#98
Webster's Dictionary Contained A Word That Didn't Exist.

For a brief period of time, *Webster's New International Dictionary* accidentally contained the word "dord," which is not an actual word. The word "dord" does not exist, but it managed to hold a place in Webster's dictionary for five years.

According to "Snopes," you could find the word in the second edition of the dictionary, which was published in 1934.

The word was situated on page 771 in between the words "Dorcopsis," meaning a type of small kangaroo, and "dore," meaning golden in color. The word "dord" was apparently a noun meaning density in physics and chemistry.

You might ask how it's possible that a non-existent word found its way into a dictionary. In 1931, there was a card bearing the notation "D or d, cont/density" that was prepared for the next edition of the dictionary.

This card was meant to indicate that the next edition should contain a listing for "D" and "d" as abbreviations of the word "density." However, this card made its way onto the word pile instead. That is how the word "dord," a synonym for density, was created.

Considering how much work and effort goes into writing, proofreading, and editing a dictionary, it's a wonder how there aren't more errors.

#99

There Is A Day Known As Brown Friday By Plumbers In America.

According to "Family Handyman," the day after Thanksgiving has been dubbed "Brown Friday" by plumbers in America. I know what you're probably thinking. There's only one reason why they would call that day "Brown Friday," but it's actually not for the reason you probably think it is.

This day after Thanksgiving is the plumber's busiest day of the year. They reportedly get a 50 percent increase in service calls. The two main reasons for the increase in service calls are jammed garbage disposals and clogged up sinks.

On Thanksgiving, everyone invites their whole family over, and they cook more food than anyone is going to be able to eat. Everybody eats more than they can, and still, there is a lot of food leftover.

Now, they need to figure out what to do with all of this extra food. Some of it is wrapped up and put in the fridge, but the rest is usually thrown down a garbage disposal. This can cause it to get jammed and clogged. Plumbers are then called out to fix this problem regularly on "Brown Friday."

The food on Thanksgiving also tends to be very greasy. After Thanksgiving, there is usually a lot of grease left sitting around. Where does this grease go? It goes down the drain.

This is not the proper way to dispose of grease, but since no one knows that, it is the common way it gets disposed of. When the hot grease makes contact with a cold pipe, it tends to solidify and clog up the drain.

This is the main reason why plumbers are called out on the day after Thanksgiving.

Rather than draining the grease down a pipe, you should let it cool down and solidify on its own before throwing it out. You could also try soaking it up with a paper towel and throwing it out.

100

Time Anxiety Is The Fear Of Being Late.

There are a lot of things for people to be anxious about these days. Social anxiety is a big one that has been troubling many young people lately. This kind of disorder should be and is taken very seriously. But have you ever heard of time anxiety? It's a very real fear of being late yourself or even of other people being late, and it is probably just as bad as social anxiety.

According to "Psychology Today," those that suffer from time anxiety feel real fear if they aren't able to arrive early for everything. Regardless of whether it's a lunch date, party, a doctor's appointment, or even an interview, they have to arrive on time or early for them all.

There may not even be any consequences from being late, but people with time anxiety will still fear it. They even fear being late for a time they have set themselves. This kind of behavior may seem strange and unreasonable, but there is a very simple explanation behind it.

The thinking is that people's fear of being late stems from their fear of death. Time anxiety can be directly related to someone's fear of running out of time or even wasting their time. They are afraid of being late just as much as they are afraid that they aren't spending the time they have properly. I think we all feel this way sometimes.

You only have a limited amount of time on this planet, and you don't want to feel as if that time is being wasted and not used the best way it can be used. This is where time anxiety stems from, not the fear of being late, but the fear of wasted time.

#101
The Largest Wave Ever Surfed Was 78 Feet Tall!

Garret McNamara wasn't expecting to break any world records the day he broke the one for the largest wave ever surfed. Up until that day, the record was held by Mike Parsons, who surfed a 77-foot tall wave in 2008 at California's Cortes Bank.

According to "Forbes," the record was broken in 2011 when McNamara took a chance and surfed a 78-foot tall wave at an obscure beach known as Nazare.

Originally the wave was thought to be 90 feet tall, but later on, it was confirmed to be only 78 feet. This was still enough for McNamara to claim the world record from Parsons.

The obscure place known as Nazare can be found about an hour from Lisbon just off the coast of Portugal. It is thought to be a dangerous place for surfers as the waves tend to break close to shore and not on distant reefs.

This means that a surfer is in danger of falling off his board too close to the shore, which could end in severe injury and even death.

McNamara went back in 2013 to surf another wave.

This one was thought to be even bigger than the 78-footer, but it has not yet been determined, so his original record still stands.

#102

In Belgium, There Is A 2-Mile Long Pipeline Used To Transport Beer.

When Xavier Vanneste, the director and heir to Bruges's only continuously working brewery De Halve Maan, first thought of a 2-mile long beer pipeline, it was just a joke or a dream. Now, that dream has become a reality.

According to "The Guardian," Vanneste first got the idea when he saw some workmen laying cables down outside his house. He rushed out onto the street to talk with them, and at that moment, he thought that it was very possible. However, laying down cables or pipes for gas is a far stretch from laying down a 2-mile long beer pipeline.

The town of Bruges is a medieval one, and its cobblestone streets and medieval buildings have secured its place on the UNESCO World Heritage list. At first, the idea was seen as foolish by Renaat Landuyt, the mayor of Bruges.

After putting some thought into it, he realized that allowing the pipeline to be built could benefit the town in many ways. The pipeline would reduce the number of beer tankers driving in and out of the town; it would ensure that the brewery remained open and provided jobs in the center of the town, and it would keep De Halve Maan, which is a historic part of the city, open and prevent the small town from being turned into a museum.

Once the mayor realized all of these benefits, it wasn't long until the building of the pipeline was approved.

The 2-mile long pipeline takes beer from the brewery within the center of town all the way to a bottling plant outside the city. It is a dream come true for many including Vanneste.

#103

There Are More Captive Tigers In The U.S. Than Wild Tigers In The World.

According to The World Wildlife Fund, there are an estimated 5,000 captive tigers in the United States alone. This exceeds the population of tigers in the wild, which is only 3,200. Only 6 percent of the captive tigers in the U.S. can be found in zoos and other such facilities.

Most of the captive tigers are found in backyards, at truck stops, sideshows, apartments, and private breeding facilities.

The lax management of captive tigers has led to an extreme bump in population numbers and an increased number of exotic pet owners, who are not only mismanaging these creatures but are also putting the lives of people and animals in danger.

In October 2011, one exotic pet owner released his many exotic pets into a local community in Ohio. This started a panic in which first responders were forced to shoot and kill more than 10 captive tigers and other animals.

In the U.S., it is actually easier to buy a tiger than it is to adopt a puppy from a shelter. People can keep a tiger on their property legally, and they are not obligated to inform their neighbors or even report it to the local officials. Keeping a tiger, which should be a wild and free creature, in the U.S. is far too easy to accomplish.

Thankfully, the WWF has called for a ban on the allowance of private ownership of tigers, and the U.S. is currently moving in the right direction.

#104

High Heels Were Originally Designed For Men In The 16th Century.

These days, it is very rare to see a lady out on the town without a good pair of heels on. They are extremely fashionable and also practical for ladies that tend to be a little on the short side. According to "Metro News," not only were high heel shoes not made for women, but they were also not made for walking.

In the 16th century, high heel shoes were first worn by Persian horsemen. The design of the shoe helped them secure their stance in stirrups. By the end of the 16th century, the Persians had started many fashion trends with the high heel for men being just one of them. Back then, the heel was seen as masculine and virile.

By the 17th century, French King Louis XIV had claimed the high heel look for himself. He was a little short, and so the heels gave him an edge. He made sure that the soles of his shoes were always painted red. Back then, this was a very expensive pigment, and it was a sign of royalty and wealth. Louis XIV ruled that only the members of his court could wear high heel shoes with a red heel. This made the shoe even more special, and imitation heels were worn.

It wasn't until the 1630s that women started wearing high heels. Women started cutting their hair short, smoking pipes, and wearing heels in order to take on the hottest male fashion trends.

Then, around the 17th century, men's and women's heels became more separated. Men's heels were made lower, thicker, and more robust, while the women's heels were taller and slimmer.

Both men and women were looking fashionable in heels until 1740; by that time, men started seeing heels as foolish, and they stopped wearing them altogether. Women also stopped wearing heels around 50 years after the French Revolution.

They only made their comeback in the mid-19th century when French pornographic pictures of women wearing heels came out. This may be the origin of the belief that heels are sexy.

105

White Cats Born With Blue Eyes Are More Likely To Be Deaf.

White cats with one or two blue eyes are very rare. They only make up about 1 to 1.5 percent of the total cat population. According to International Cat Care, an autosomal-dominant gene, which has been called the "W (for white) gene," is the gene responsible for these traits. This gene is pleiotropic, which means it has more than one effect.

This gene in a cat is responsible for giving the cat white fur, blue eyes, and causing deafness. There is a strong link between white cats with blue eyes and deaf cats because of this gene. However, if you have a white cat with blue eyes, you don't have to worry because not all of them will be deaf. This outcome in the cat is also dependent on other genes in the cat and/or environmental factors.

If a white cat has two blue eyes, then it is 3 to 5 times more likely to be a deaf cat than a cat with only one blue eye or a cat with no blue eyes. A white cat with one blue eye is twice as likely to be deaf as a cat with no blue eyes. Also, cats with long white hair are three times more likely to be deaf bilaterally, which means they are deaf in both ears.

Natural selection is not very friendly to white cats that also have blue eyes. Besides the fact that they are more likely to be deaf, because of their blue eyes, they have reduced vision in low light, and they are photophobic.

This is why you won't find a lot of feral white cats with blue eyes, but due to breeding selection, they tend to make very popular pets.

#106
On Average, Americans Own Seven Pairs Of Blue Jeans.

It's fair to say that almost everyone owns a pair of jeans that they love wearing more than any other clothing item they have.

They fit perfectly, they feel comfortable, they aren't too hot or too cold, and they make you look good. No one would argue with you if you said that blue jeans are the best.

Just how obsessed are we with blue jeans? Jeans are especially popular in America, where everyone is proud to say that they grew up in denim, and according to "CNN," Americans, on average, own about seven pairs of blue jeans.

Denim jeans first started out as workwear for hard labor, mostly down in the mines or out on fields and factories. They were made baggy and strong to endure such labor.

The fit and shape of denim jeans started to slim down in the 1980s when high fashion brands started introducing the idea of designer jeans.

Today, the United States consumers purchase approximately 450 million pairs of jeans each year, and it's estimated that each American citizen owns seven pairs of blue jeans, one for each day of the week.

However, it's thought that out of the seven pairs, women only wear about four of them.

#107
There Is A Breathable Liquid You Can't Drown In.

We've seen it done in sci-fi movies all the time. Someone will be introduced to a type of liquid that they can breathe in. First, they will panic, but eventually, they'll realize that they can breathe just fine in this futuristic or alien liquid. It happens the same in all the movies. However, what if this breathable liquid isn't just fantasy and there is actually some fact behind it?

According to "Zidbits," breathable liquid does exist. For a liquid that allows us to breathe to work, it needs to be able to do two things. It needs to supply oxygen to our lungs as well as remove carbon dioxide. Around the 1960s, scientists were experimenting with perfluorinated hydrocarbons, which is a liquid that is able to dissolve both carbon dioxide and oxygen with ease.

The best version of this liquid is known as LiquiVent, or by its scientific name perflubron. It is an oily, clear liquid that is capable of holding nearly twice as much oxygen as air can. It is twice as dense as water and has a low boiling point, so it can easily be removed from the lungs by evaporation. This breathable liquid is also inert, which means it can't damage the lungs.

While this liquid, or versions of it, has been used in movies for deep-sea diving, that is not its main use. Its main use is, of course, medicinal.

This kind of liquid is very useful for people who have breathing problems or lung defects. For instance, premature babies often have underdeveloped lungs, and it's very easy for their lungs to collapse.

The perflubron can help these premature babies breathe until their lungs have fully developed. It almost recreates the conditions the baby had while it was in the womb while safely delivering oxygen to the baby until it is ready to breathe on its own.

#108

The First Bumper Car Company Was Named Dodgem And For A Good Reason.

Bumper cars are probably one of the best pastimes for unleashing all of that pent-up energy we gather during the day. They're simple and fun. Anyone can get the hang of a bumper car. But did you know that the first bumper cars made were not meant to collide with each other? According to "Pin Stack," the first bumper cars were made with the intent for drivers to purposefully try to avoid each other in all the chaos.

Bumper cars were first introduced by a company called Dodgem in the early 1920s. The rides have grown in popularity ever since then. The whole point of bumper cars today is to bump into each other. You want to ram into your opponents as hard as you possibly can.

When bumper cars were first introduced, the whole point of the game was to try your hardest to avoid colliding with the other cars. This is why the first company and cars that were introduced were named Dodgem.

The reason why bumper cars were not supposed to actually bump into each other is actually pretty simple. They wouldn't have survived the collision. Back then, the cars were so fragile that a single collision could break the car or make it fall to pieces.

A single kick could dent the side of a car. The cars were often nailed back together and dents were hammered out at the end of each day. This is probably because the first bumper cars were constructed of tin, a very flimsy and fragile metal.

When they were first introduced, the thrill of bumper cars came from avoiding the cars speeding toward you in mass chaos. Now, the thrill comes from banging into every single car and making sure the driver will feel it the next morning.

109

Dentistry Is One Of The Oldest Medical Professions In History.

Dentistry is one of many important medical professions. We've all heard tales of how in the past, people's teeth were yellow, rotten, and decaying because there were no dentists. However, recent evidence has shown that there may have been dentists before there were doctors.

According to the American Dental Education Association, the first mention of the profession can be dated as far back as 7000 B.C. The evidence found from 7000 B.C. is sparse and not very descriptive, but evidence found from 5000 B.C. provides more information. They found some Sumerian text that explained how tooth worms are the cause of dental decay. This idea, although obviously false, was not proven so until the 1700s.

In ancient Greece, they were writing about dentistry and tooth decay, but the first book that was entirely devoted to dentistry was only published in 1530. This book was called *The Little Medicinal Book for All Kinds of Diseases and Infirmities of the Teeth*. Even after this big leap in the world of dentistry, it only became an established profession in the 1700s.

Pierre Fauchard, a French surgeon also known as the father of dentistry, published an influential book about the profession in 1723. The book, *The Surgeon Dentist, a Treatise on Teeth*, defined a full and comprehensive system for treating and caring for teeth for the first time.

He was the one who first identified that the acids from sugar led to tooth decay, and he introduced dental fillings and dental prosthesis for the first time.

Since then, the dentistry profession has grown, with the first dental college being established in 1840, and by 1873, Colgate had mass-produced the first toothpaste and toothbrushes. Dentistry may be the oldest medical profession, but it was also the slowest at developing.

#110
Octopuses Don't Touch Each Other Unless Fighting Or Mating.

Octopuses are probably the most antisocial creatures in the ocean. They see their own kind as either competition or food, and the only reason for them to touch is for fighting or mating. A male octopus's one goal in life is to spread its genes on to the next generation of octopus, but this simple-sounding task is a very dangerous and life-threatening one for the males. According to "BBC Earth," female octopuses tend to strangle and eat male octopuses either during or after mating.

You've probably heard of this kind of thing happening in the wild before. The female praying mantis is known to bite the head off of its mate when she is done with him. The female octopus is unique in that they are the only creatures to do so during the act of mating instead of afterward. Female octopuses are often bigger and stronger than male octopuses, so it's not a difficult thing for them to do.

The way an octopus mates is quite intimate given the nature of the species. The male literally places his mating arm, which is just like all his other arms but with a central groove that packets of spermatophores are released into, inside the female and releases the sperm inside of her. This puts the male in a very vulnerable position with the female, but in order to pass the sperm into the female, they have to stay in this position for a few minutes to half an hour.

The male does have a few tricks in order to avoid being eaten by the female during mating. They can sneak into the female's den disguised as another female.

They sometimes try to mate at an arm's length, literally. They are known to also sacrifice their whole mating arm to the female and retreat. Seems like quite a lot of effort just to get a few offspring.

#111
The United States Wrote A Check And Purchased Alaska From Russia.

Have you ever wondered how much a state or country would be worth? Do you ever think about how much you would be able to buy a country for? Well, if you had the money, you could have purchased Alaska for $7.2 million back in 1867. According to the Library of Congress, William H. Seward, the secretary of state, purchased Alaska from Russia on March 30, 1867, by signing a check for $7.2 million.

At the time, Alaska was a land that was mostly unexplored, and most thought it was a joke to buy it. Critics called the secretary of state crazy, and he was laughed at for spending so much money on what was known as "Seward's icebox."

Alaska was very large, and the purchase of it would increase the size of the United States by 20 percent.

The Russians had tried to sell the land to the U.S. back when President James Buchanan was in power, but then the Civil War put the negotiations on hold.

After the war, Seward had a hard time convincing the Senate that buying Alaska was a good move. He did his best to show them how Alaska would be an important addition to the United States, and he eventually won the approval by one vote.

It turned out that buying Alaska was an extremely good move for the United States after they discovered gold there in the 1880s and 1990s.

#112

The Car Company, Volkswagen, Has Sold More Sausages Than Cars.

The biggest car company in Germany also has a side business where they sell currywurst, a sausage with a spicy sauce. According to "The Local," Volkswagen sausage sales were higher than their car sales in 2015. They sold 7.3 million currywurst in 2015, and they only sold 6.3 million cars in the same year.

It's not clear whether or not their sausage sales have outdone their car sales in previous years. Although the car company sold more sausages than cars that year, the cars did bring in more profit than the sausages did.

The Volkswagen company has hit rocky times since it was revealed that their diesel cars were built with emission-cheating software. The environmental authorities in the U.S. were the ones that discovered this, and the scandal is still traveling around the globe. At least they have their sausage side company to fall back on if the car side doesn't work out.

#113

Snakes Can Be Used To Predict Earthquakes.

China is one of the few places on earth that is constantly being struck by earthquakes. Some of the earthquakes are large, and most of them are small, but all can be devastating if you're not prepared. Most of the earthquakes hit small rural areas, but it's not unlikely for a big city to be hit by one.

The city of Tangshan was struck by an earthquake in 1976 that killed about 250,000 people and destroyed most of the city. Thankfully, Chinese scientists say they have developed a way to perhaps predict these earthquakes days before they hit.

According to "The Independent," they have discovered that snakes have the ability to predict an earthquake from 75 miles away. This means that they can detect an earthquake at least 5 days before it hits. The director of the earthquake bureau in Nanning, Jiang Weisong, says that snakes will act very erratically if they sense an oncoming earthquake.

He has observed them moving out of their nests, even when hibernating from the cold, and squirming to get to safety. If a snake has sensed a big earthquake, it will even throw itself head-first into walls while trying to escape. This erratic behavior is uncommon in snakes, so it's pretty easy to notice. When they start acting this way, then they know that an earthquake is on its way.

At the moment, scientists are monitoring snakes on snake farms using hidden video cameras that are connected to a broadband internet connection. This runs 24 hours a day, so they won't miss anything. This system allows them to observe the snakes in their natural habitat so any kind of behavior won't be influenced by anyone's presence.

Nanning is only 1 of 12 Chinese cities with this snake monitoring system, and it has over 143 animal monitoring units active. This will help them better predict and prepare for any future earthquakes that could hit the city.

#114
The Great Mongol Leader Has Over 16 Million Descendants.

Genghis Khan was the Great Mongol Leader who lived between the years 1162 and 1227. The Mongol armies would raid and attack many small villages and towns. The men always shared their spoils among themselves, including food, gold, and other things. They shared it all, except for one thing: the women. It's a well-known rule that all the most beautiful women belonged to Genghis Khan. He is famous for being an enthusiastic lover and having many wives and children.

According to "The Guardian," the Great Mongol Leader might have had a lot more offspring than we originally thought.

Recent genetic studies in central Asia have revealed that Genghis Khan has around 16 million male descendants today. About 1 in every 200 men alive is a relative of the Mongol Leader.

They were able to determine this by looking at the Y chromosome in several different men. The Y chromosome is the gene that turns an embryo into a male, and it is a genetic package that is only passed on from father to son. Y chromosomes that belong to different men usually vary slightly, so you are able to tell the difference between each individual man.

The scientist took tissue samples from 2,000 different men, and through testing, they found that a huge amount of them showed no differences at all. The only plausible explanation for this is that they are all related.

The researchers dug deeper and found that all of the people who shared this chromosome match the spread of Genghis's empire. His empire spread from China to the Middle East, and so do the people who share this chromosome. It's not extremely hard to believe that a man who slept with the most beautiful woman in his empire could have left behind such a large legacy.

#115
Coca-Cola Was The First Soft Drink Consumed In Space.

On July 12, 1985, Coca-Cola became the first soft drink to be consumed by astronauts in space. It beat Pepsi by only eight hours. On that day, the space shuttle, Challenger, was launched into space with a new can of Coca-Cola and a new can of Pepsi on board.

Both companies had filled out an application to have their drinks tested on the space shuttle, and it was up to the astronauts to decide whose drink they would test first.

According to "Soda Pop Craft," they chose to test Coca-Cola first only because the company had submitted its application a little before Pepsi had.

The reason for having this test was interesting. Drinking soda in space sounds like a great idea until you remember the fact that the drinks are carbonated. Carbonated drinks and space just don't mix.

Both Coca-Cola and Pepsi had to design all new cans for their drinks so that the drinks tasted the same but weren't as carbonated. This was so the sodas didn't explode while on the shuttle. Coca-Cola went with a type of screw-top lid, while Pepsi went with a pop-top lid. Both designs did the trick, and none of them exploded.

The test was done so NASA could see if the sugary beverages reacted any differently to our taste buds while in space. Unfortunately, no new discoveries were made that day. In fact, the astronauts gave mixed reviews on both sodas, so NASA decided not to include any of them in the space shuttle food pantries in the future.

#116
Put A Pillow On Your Fridge Day Really Exists.

May 29 is officially Put a Pillow on Your Fridge Day! According to "The Fact Site," the holiday is celebrated every year in the U.S. and Europe. Put a Pillow on Your Fridge Day is all about celebrating good fortune and prosperity, and having some fun while doing it.

The actual origin of the holiday can be dated back all the way to the early 1900s. On this day, families would place a piece of torn off cloth or linen inside their larder, which was a cold closet or room in which they stored their meat and provisions, kind of like a refrigerator.

The cloth was often torn off of a blanket or gown. It was believed that this brought prosperity, good fortune, rich fertility, and the possibility of plentiful food to their house. Today, the age-old holiday is celebrated by putting a pillow on top of your fridge for the whole day. It's a fun way to keep the tradition alive and bring good fortune to you and your house.

#117
Chocolate Milk Comes From Brown Cows.

Chocolate milk doesn't actually come from brown cows, but that's what 7 percent of American adults believe. According to "The Washington Post," an online nationally represented survey that was commissioned by the Innovation Center of U.S. Dairy showed these results. About 7 percent of all American adults believed that chocolate milk came from brown cows.

That's around 16.4 million people who are misinformed. All of them are unaware that chocolate milk is actually milk mixed with sugar, cocoa, and other additives.

This kind of information has brought to light what observers in agriculture, nutrition, and education have been saying for decades: Too many Americans are agriculturally illiterate. This means that they aren't properly informed as to where food is grown, how it is grown, and what is in it. In the early 1990s, a Department of Agriculture study found that 1 in every 5 adults in America didn't even know that hamburgers were made from beef.

Most people are uneducated when it comes to where

food comes from, how it is grown, how it gets to the store, and all the other processes in between. This is because there is something lacking in the education system. People are hard-wired to know that if they need anything food-related, they just go to the store. They aren't informed on anything else beyond that. This kind of education is seen as normal since most people who aren't agriculturally informed aren't part of the business themselves.

The belief is that they don't plan on getting involved in the system, so they don't need to know anything about it. The only question to ask now is this: Is that the right sort of thinking to have on the subject?

#118
A Kangaroo Can't Hop Without Its Tail.

Kangaroos are large and very loveable creatures, thanks to characters like Kanga from "Winnie the Pooh." And while they're easily identifiable, they have plenty of strange facts that will surprise you.

According to "The Fact Site," a kangaroo's tail acts as a third leg for them. If you lift their tail off the ground, they won't be able to balance or hop. A kangaroo doesn't walk. When they hop, they are, in a way, walking, and they use both of their legs and their tail to do this unique walking movement of theirs.

They push off the ground with their tail first, followed quickly by jumping with their legs. Along with this, they use their tail for balancing, so if you were to lift a kangaroo's tail off of the floor, it won't be able to balance itself, and it won't be able to hop.

That's just one of the many unique facts about kangaroos. Did you also know that kangaroos are the largest mammals that walk by hopping? Kangaroos hop because they have to. Kangaroos' legs are structured so they can't move independently from each other. The only way they can move is by hopping forward because they're legs are structurally incapable of performing a walking motion.

This obviously doesn't affect them as they can hop at speeds up to 35 miles an hour! Speaking of hopping forward, a kangaroo can't move backward because its big, muscular tail prevents it from doing so. Its only way is forward, which doesn't seem that bad.

With all of these facts under your belt, you probably want to go have a look at the loveable creatures yourself. If you do, remember that male kangaroos are called boomers, females are called flyers, and the babies are called joeys.

#119
The Time Rabbits Attacked Napoleon And Won.

Some of the details of this day are a bit fuzzy, but most of them seem to correspond, and they are extremely funny. According to "Mental Floss," Napoleon's greatest defeat was not at Waterloo but eight years earlier when he was attacked and forced to flee by a horde of rabbits.

It happened in July 1807, just after the Treaties of Tilsit was signed by Napoleon. This ended the war between Imperial Russia and the French Empire. As a celebration, the emperor suggested a rabbit hunt, and Alexandre Berthier, Napoleon's chief of staff, made it happen. He arranged for there to be an outdoor luncheon, collected a whole colony of rabbits, and invited the military's biggest brass to join. The story here gets a bit fuzzy, as some accounts say that he collected hundreds of rabbits, while others say it was as many as 3,000. We'll just say that there were a lot of rabbits. Berthier had them caged along the edges of a grass-covered field.

The hunt was on. Napoleon and some beaters and gun bearers started their prowl, and the rabbits were released from their cages. This is where you would expect the rabbits to scurry in fear, but instead, they charged straight toward Napoleon. Hundreds of rabbits jumped at his legs and tried to jump higher on to his jacket. At first, the men had a good laugh about it, but their laughs stopped, and they grew more serious about the situation.

According to stories of the day, the rabbits swarmed around the emperor's legs. Napoleon tried to shoo them with his riding crop, and the men cracked whips and grabbed sticks to scare the creatures off. The rabbits didn't seem bothered by these attempts and carried on with their attack. Eventually, Napoleon had to retreat to his coach, but even then, the rabbits chased after him. They allegedly flanked left and right around Napoleon's men and chased him all the way to the coach. The onslaught only ceased once the emperor had successfully made his retreat as the coach drove away from the rabbits.

Instead of wild rabbits, Berthier had gotten a whole bunch of tamed farm rabbits. They didn't see Napoleon as a hunter but rather as the man who brought them food each day. He was essentially a waiter to them.

#120
A Japanese Engineer Survived Two Atomic Bombs.

There were two atomic bomb attacks during World War II. One hit Hiroshima, and the other hit Nagasaki. It's estimated that 260,000 people survived the attacks; however, according to "History.com," only a few managed to survive both attacks. Tsutomu Yamaguchi was one of those few.

Yamaguchi was a Japanese engineer working for Mitsubishi Heavy Industries and was in Hiroshima on a three-month-long business trip. August 6, 1945, was supposed to be his last day, but around 8:15 that morning, he heard an aircraft fly over him. He looked up and saw the American B-29 bomber drop a small object that was connected to a parachute over the city. In a sudden white flash, the sky erupted in a blaze of light. The shock wave sent Yamaguchi flying through the air and threw him into a potato patch. He was less than 2 miles away from ground zero.

The skin on his face and arms was burned badly, and his eardrums were ruptured. On August 7, he made his way to the train station, which was still working, and made the long journey to his hometown of Nagasaki where his wife and infant son were waiting for him.

He arrived in Nagasaki on August 8 and went straight to the doctor. They treated his burns as best they could, and he was sent home. The burns were so bad that his mother didn't even recognize him, and his wife accused him of being a ghost. He went to bed, and the next morning, August 9, he dragged himself to work.

At around 11 a.m., he was in his boss's office when the second bomb dropped. Thanks to the design of the office he was in, he managed to surface from the blast relatively unharmed.

His wife and child were out buying burn ointment for him at the time and took refuge from the blast inside a tunnel. If they weren't out for that reason, they would have been at home right in the middle of the blast area, and they wouldn't have survived.

Yamaguchi believes this was all an act of fate. If he hadn't been involved in the first bomb that hit Hiroshima, then his wife wouldn't have been out buying him burn ointment, and they would have died in the second bombing.

#121

The Record For Highest Fall Without A Parachute Is 33,333 Feet.

Vesna Vulovic was a stewardess for Yugoslav Airlines when the plane she was working on exploded mid-air on January 20, 1972.

According to "BBC News," all 27 passengers and crew died except for her. Vesna was trapped in the tail end of the plane by a food cart.

That section of the plane plummeted to earth with her inside it. The section hit a wooded and snow-blanketed area in the mountains, and this is believed to be the reason why she survived the fall. The snow and woods cushioned the impact, but she didn't come away unharmed. After being rescued by a woodsman who heard her screaming, she was sent to the hospital. She fell into a coma for 10 days.

She had two crushed vertebrae, a fractured skull, several broken ribs, two broken legs, and a broken pelvis. She recovered from the accident, and after a brief period of being paralyzed from the waist down, she returned to work at a desk job at the airline.Her fall earned her a place in the Guinness Book of Records in 1985 for the highest fall survived without a parachute.

#122

In 1943, U.S. Officials Banned Sliced Bread.

Sliced bread first came out in 1928, and it was a hit among the public. It was called "the greatest forward step in the baking industry since bread was wrapped." However, during World War II, this step forward was halted for a brief period of time.

According to "The Vintage News," Claude R. Wickard, the secretary of Agriculture and the head of the War Foods Administration, decided to ban sliced bread in America. He came up with the idea and pushed the ban through all in the same year. The reason for the ban is unclear, although it was probably an effort to save resources such as wheat, wax paper, and steel, all of which were used in the production of sliced bread.

Sliced bread was very popular in the U.S. at the time, so you can imagine the outrage that came from the ban of it. Thankfully, the ban only lasted three months. On March 8, 1943, Wickard rescinded the ban and said that the savings from it were not as much as he expected them to be.

123

Finding Water On Mars As An April Fool's Prank.

Every April Fool's Day, which is the first day of every April, we all try our hardest to prank and pun each other. All this is done for fun and laughter. According to "Universe Today," not even big science hotshots like NASA are above a few harmless pranks. Never was this more obvious than in 2005, when NASA pranked the world about finding water on Mars.

On March 31, 2005, a teaser was posted on NASA's Astronomy Picture of the Day website. It was titled "Water on Mars!" with a presentation to follow the next day, on April 1. This left people ecstatic.

This was an incredible find for the human race. If there was water on Mars, then that meant there could have been life on Mars at one stage. Science was about to make a huge leap forward. The next day, April 1, 2005, NASA posted their presentation of water on Mars, and it left the whole world either in tears or crying from laughter. Their presentation was a picture of a glass of water standing on top of two Mars chocolate bars. It was water on Mars, but not the kind that everyone was hoping for.

#124
A Cat Is The Mayor Of A Historical District In Alaska.

A small town in Alaska called Talkeetna, with a population of only 900 residents, had the most unusual mayor. A cat named Stubbs, or Mayor Stubbs, as the cat was mostly known, was the mayor for about 20 years.

According to "The Guardian," the yellow feline was elected mayor of the town in 1998 in a write-in campaign. Stories say that Stubbs liked to prowl the town looking for attention and that he enjoyed drinking water laced with catnip out of a margarita glass.

Understandably, the cat became an instant tourist attraction. Stubbs even survived an attack from a dog in 2013. By late 2016, Stubbs was an old cat, and instead of prowling the town, he rested at home most days. Sadly, Stubbs died after 20 years and 3 months of being mayor of the small town in Alaska. He lived a long life, and he will be missed by his people. It's said that one of his owner's kittens, Denali, is ready to walk in Stubbs's footsteps and take over his duties as mayor.

#125
The Police Followed A Giant To Make Sure He Didn't Fall On Anyone.

Andre the Giant is known by several nicknames, including "The Greatest Drunk on Earth." Andre stood at 7 feet, 4 inches tall, 550 pounds, and was capable of drinking an amount of alcohol that would kill any normal-sized person. According to "All That's Interesting," Andre the Giant once drank 108 12-ounce beers while waiting at an airport with Hulk Hogan. It's believed that his tolerance to alcohol was so strong that he could drink several bottles of wine before even feeling a bit tipsy.

A story, told by Andre's "The Princess Bride" co-star Cary Elwes, recounts a night when Andre was so drunk that he fell over on a man while waiting for a cab in New York. Apparently, the man was badly hurt. This caused the New York Police Department to send undercover cops to follow Andre while he was in the city to make sure that he didn't get drunk and fall over on someone again. This was, of course, all a story told by Elwes, and it hasn't been proven true yet. Although, I wouldn't put it past them.

#126
Crocodiles Can't Stick Their Tongues Out!

Who hasn't stuck their tongue out at someone once? I know I did it when I was a kid, and I'm pretty sure almost everyone did it during some silly argument over whose turn it was on the swings. Well, a crocodile will have to find some other way of teasing his opponent during an argument because crocodiles can't stick their tongues out at all.

According to "Metro News," a crocodile's tongue is held in place on the roof of its mouth by a membrane. This ensures that the tongue doesn't move, and it makes it easier for crocodiles to press food against the top of their mouth to crush it. It also means that a crocodile is unable to move its tongue outside of its mouth at all. This can come in quite handy when a crocodile snaps its jaws shut.

They are able to snap their mouth closed so fast that they might bite their own tongue off it was able to move out of the mouth. This little design can be found in American crocodiles, dwarf crocodiles, mugger crocodiles, and Nile crocodiles.

#127
A Woman Tried To Commit Suicide, But The Wind Said "Nope."

Fate is a funny thing, and it gets its work done in mysterious ways. Elvita Adams, a 29-year-old woman, witnessed the true power of fate when she tried to commit suicide in 1979.

According to "The New York Times," Elvita tried to jump off the 86th floor of the Empire State Building late one night.

A fall from that height would kill anyone, but fate had other plans for Elvita. It's suspected that when Elvita jumped from the 86th-floor observation deck, a strong gust of wind blew her back toward the building and landed her on a three-foot ledge on the 85th floor of the building.

The night supervisor, George Reice, said that one of the building's guards heard Elvita's cries for help and found her at 8:15 on the 85th-floor ledge.

Elvita was sent to the hospital with nothing more than a fractured pelvis. At the time, there were usually four guards stationed on the 86th-floor observation deck, which is surrounded by an iron spiked fence that is eight feet tall, but no one saw Elvita jump.

It was obvious to police that this was an attempted suicide, and it was lucky for Elvita that the wind intervened where no one else could.

#128

The Chinese Police Use Geese As Watchdogs.

In the rural parts of China's Xinjiang Province, the police are starting to turn to geese to stand guard at their stations instead of watchdogs. The geese are trained and stationed as guards, and according to National Geographic, it's working like a charm. A report was filed of an attempted break-in at one of the police stations.

A man tried to break in and steal back his bike that was confiscated by the police. The guard geese heard the intrusion and sounded the alarm, waking up the sleeping police officers and stopping the intruder in his tracks.

You may be asking yourself why use geese when dogs are probably less complicated. Well, the truth is that geese are actually less complicated to train and easier to care for. The director of bird conservation at Audubon Connecticut, Patrick Cumins, says that geese have better hearing and sight than both humans and dogs and they are very territorial.

They're easy to care for as they are satisfied eating cracked corn or grazing on grass. They don't need to be trained to guard a certain area because it is a basic instinct for them. They instinctively protect their territory and their flock, their flock being the police officers or anyone in a police uniform.

Geese, unlike dogs, can't be easily distracted by food or treats, and so an intruder would have a hard time getting past one without sounding the alarm.

All in all, geese make excellent guard dogs.

#129
The Pig War.

The war known as "The Pig War" is probably one of the weirdest disputes in American and British history. The only blood that was spilled during this war belonged to a pig. According to "Historic U.K.," this story begins back in 1846.

It was this year that the Oregon Treaty was signed between Britain and the U.S., which aimed to put a stop to the border disputes between the United States and British North America, known today as Canada.

One island called San Juan became a problem during the treaty as both the U.S. and the U.K. claimed sovereignty over it.

Citizens from both countries began settling on the island. It's suggested that both sets of citizens actually got along with each other until one day when a pig wandered onto the land of American settler Lyman Cutlar.

The pig was owned by Charles Griffin, a British employee of the Hudson Bay Company. When Cutlar saw the pig on his property, it was eating his potatoes. Cutlar lost his temper and shot and killed the pig. Griffin was not happy about the death of his pig, and even though Cutlar offered him $10 in compensation for the pig, Griffin refused the payment and reported Cutlar to the local British authorities.

Long story short, the American citizens on the island drew up a petition requesting protection from the U.S. Military.

It started with the U.S. sending a 66-man company to the island; the British responded by sending three British warships in order to show force. There was a month-long standoff between the two militaries when, finally, James Douglas, the governor of British Columbia, ordered Admiral Robert L. Baynes to land his troops on the island and attack the American troops. Thankfully, Baynes refused the orders, saying that he would not "involve two great nations in a war over a squabble about a pig."

By this time, word had gotten back to Washington and London of the dispute. They were shocked to hear that 84 guns, 3 warships, and 2,600 men were involved in a dispute over a pig. Negotiations started, and it was declared that both countries should have no more than 100 men on the island at the time.

The war only ended in 1872 when Kaiser Wilhelm I of Germany led an international commission that decided the island should fall completely under American control. This was the end of the Pig War, whose only victim was a small pig.

#130
Cows Have Accents!

According to "BBC News," cows moo with regional accents. The farmers in Somerset were the first to notice that their cows sounded different from other cows. The farmers were able to hear the difference in their cows' moos because of the close bond they have with the herd. It's the same with dogs; if you have a close enough bond with your dog, you would be able to recognize their bark from another dog's bark.

John Wells, a professor of phonetics at the University of London, said the same thing has been seen in birds. You would be able to hear a distinctly different chirp in birds of the same species that come from different regions.

Dr. Jeanine Treffers-Daller, a reader in linguistics at the University of the West of England in Bristol, said that a cow's accent could be influenced by its relatives. In the same way we learn how to speak from our parents, a cow would learn how to speak from its parents and the herd. This can lead to each herd having its own distinct sound.

EPILOGUE

Hi, dear reader, I'm the author, Larry Baz.

I want to thank you for choosing and reading this book. Hope you enjoyed it and had a great time.

If you don't mind, I would like to ask you for a favor, *"Can you help me leave a honest review about this book on Amazon?"*

That will help me to create better books in the future because I really care about every reader's feelings and feedback, and I will read every review of my book.

And leaving a honest review also can help people to know whether this book is what they want or not. Your sincere opinion can help them a lot.

Very appreciate your kind assistance!

Best,

-Larry Baz

INDEX

www.ingramcontent.com/pod-product-compliance
Lightning Source LLC
Chambersburg PA
CBHW031059250726

48655CB00004B/1513